What Should We Tell Our Children About Vietnam?

What Should We Tell Our Children About Vietnam?

Bill McCloud

University of Oklahoma Press : Norman and London

McCloud, Bill, 1948–
   What should we tell our children about Vietnam? / by Bill McCloud.—
1st ed.
   p.   cm.
   ISBN: O-8061-2229-3 (alk. paper)
   1. Vietnamese Conflict, 1961–1975.   I. Title.
DS557.7.M4   1989
959.704'3—dc20   89-40218
                                                                        CIP

The paper in this book meets the guidelines for permanence and durability
of the Committee on Production Guidelines for Book Longevity of the Council on Library Resources, Inc. ∞

For my mother and the memory of my father
and for
Tracy and our children, Cassy and Matt

The war is . . . beginning all over again for the children of the Vietnam War generation, who now seek to know just what happened to our nation in the turbulent 1960s and 1970s.

Walter Capps, 1982

If Vietnam is to leave any useful legacy, America owes it to itself to make a fair assessment of the lessons of that tragedy.

Henry Kissinger, 1985

Contents

Myra MacPherson
Ben Maddalena
Thomas H. Moorer
John D. Negroponte
Donald Oberdorfer,
  Jr.
Lawrence F. O'Brien
Tim O'Brien
Charlton Ogburn, Jr.
George S. Patton
Tom Paxton
Jeff Perez
Ed Perkins
John Clark Pratt
Nicholas Proffitt
Thomas R. Pullen
Mr. and Mrs. Ed
  Pulliam
Allen Repp
Elliot L. Richardson
William P. Rogers

Lionel Rosenblatt
Dean Rusk
Pierre Salinger
Harrison Salisbury
Neta Sanders
Arthur Schlesinger,
  Jr.
R. L. Schreadley
Pete Seeger
Paul Shannon
Evelyn Sloat
Lillian M. Snyder
Theodore Sorensen
Shelby L. Stanton
Jerold Starr
James Stockdale
Oliver Stone
Mary Stout
Harry G. Summers,
  Jr.
Sherry Svoboda

Howard N. Tanner
Telford Taylor
Garry Trudeau
William Tuohy
Kurt Vonnegut
John Waghelstein
Frank Walker
Paul C. Warnke
James H. Webb, Jr.
Caspar W.
  Weinberger
Spencer Welch
William C.
  Westmoreland
Robert Wilson
Ronald L. Ziegler
E. R. Zumwalt, Jr.

Acknowledgments

Many people deserve thanks for the encouragement and assistance they gave me during the development of this project.

Charlton Ogburn was the first person to convince me that my letters were of national interest. Richard Snow proved that Mr. Ogburn was right. Tom Radko and Patricia Dornbusch, my editors at the University of Oklahoma Press, turned the letters into a book. My wife encouraged me during every phase.

I also would like to thank Larry Burdick, Ph.D., Superintendent of the Pryor, Oklahoma, Public Schools; Bud Osborne, Assistant Superintendent; Rick Elliott, Principal of Pryor Junior High School; and the faculty, staff, and students at Pryor Junior High.

A special thanks to my second hour American history class of the 1987–88 school year. We shared an incredible year. One I think we'll never forget.

Finally, a word about the letters. The 128 letters presented here are all reprinted with the permission of their writers. Editing was kept to a minimum; most are reprinted in their entirety, although extraneous material was deleted and some were shortened slightly. The biographical information about the contributors was obtained either from the contributors or from *Who's Who in America*. I offer my heartfelt thanks to all the people who were willing to answer my question. Their answers make up this book.

Bill McCloud

Pryor, Oklahoma

Introduction

In February of 1987 my principal and friend, Rick Elliott, told me that he wanted the Vietnam War to be covered more thoroughly than it had been in the social studies classes at our junior high school in Pryor, Oklahoma. Although Vietnam was our nation's most recent war, America's combat role in it had ended before most of our students were born. When you consider that the war was the most divisive event in the past hundred years of our history, it becomes obvious that it is something that desperately needs to be taught in our schools.

I was especially interested in the subject because of my personal history. In 1967, I was attending my first year of college and living at home with my family, in Ponca City, Oklahoma. I rode to school each day in a car pool with four of my friends from high school. While on the way one day, someone in the car mentioned that he thought it would be exciting, maybe even fun, if we just dropped out of college and joined the army. The driver turned the car around in the middle of the highway. We drove back home and eventually stood together as a group to be inducted into the U.S. Army.

I enlisted in the army knowing that I would almost certainly end up in Vietnam. While I understood that we were fighting to keep Communists from taking over the government of South Vietnam, I had no sophisticated knowledge of the real causes of the war or how things had gotten to the point they were at in late 1967.

I served in Vietnam from March of 1968 through March of 1969 as the flight operations coordinator (specialist fifth class) for the 147th Assault Support Helicopter Company, based near the coastal city of Vung Tau. Our nickname was the "Hillclimbers," and our motto was "Press On." We had more than a dozen Chinook helicopters in our company, and my job was to stay at base operations and maintain communications with the helicopters while they were on their missions. During my off-duty time I was able to go along on many missions as we flew in support of the ground combat troops who were actually engaging the enemy. I flew on missions during my off-duty hours for the excitement involved. In one of the letters that I wrote to my mother I told her that I thought going on helicopter missions during the Vietnam War must be the last great adventure on earth.

Although there was never a dull moment while I was in Vietnam, I was more amazed by and interested in the war that seemed to be going on back in America. While I was in Vietnam there was a week-long takeover by students of several buildings at Columbia University; Dr. Martin Luther King, Jr., and Senator Robert F. Kennedy were assassinated; Dr. Benjamin Spock was found guilty of conspiracy (the verdict was later overturned); and Chicago became the scene of the most violent national party convention in American history, as antiwar demonstrators clashed with police. From my perspective, the Vietnam War seemed to be going on in America, too.

After leaving the service in 1970, I pushed the memories of my Vietnam experience into the back of my mind, and I do not remember thinking much about the war until the spring of 1985, when I met Thomas Boettcher. He was a Vietnam veteran from my hometown of Ponca City, Oklahoma, and his book, *Vietnam: The Valor and the Sorrow*, had just been published. It was the first book I had bought about the Vietnam War, and as I read it, I found myself thinking for the first time of the conflict as history.

By February of 1987, I had been teaching junior high school social studies for twelve years but had never discussed the Vietnam War in the classroom. Now that I was faced with the task, I felt uncomfortable with it, not because my experiences during the war had been traumatic, but because I had no idea how or what to teach about it.

I knew that my teaching would have to include more than just an anecdotal personal history. I could tell my students about the army training me for three months for a job I was then never assigned to do. I could tell them about the free mail privilege, which meant I could send as many letters home as I wanted without ever using a postage stamp. I could try to describe the sound made by Russian .122 rockets as they hit the airfield. I could talk about the exciting day I got to meet entertainer Ann-Margret. I could tell what it was like to spend seven days in Sydney, Australia, and then have to return to Vietnam. I could tell them about the day the helicopter I was riding in made a series of direct combat assaults over a period of fifteen and a half hours. I could talk about the importance of the short-timer's calendar. Those things might be of some interest, but there would have to be more.

To prepare myself for teaching my eighth-grade students about the Vietnam War, I started by sending surveys to sixty Oklahoma junior high school principals, hoping to find out the grade level at which the war was usually taught, how much time was spent covering it, and the number of veterans involved in teaching it. I wanted to discover the status of Vietnam War education in Oklahoma junior high schools so that I could see where my own course would fit in.

Thirty-five percent of the principals who responded reported that the war was not taught at all in their schools. Three of those principals thought the war was a more appropriate subject to teach in high school. When taught in junior high schools, it was usually taught as part of an eighth-grade American history class, with one or two weeks devoted to it. In my survey, 12 percent of those teaching about the war were Vietnam veterans.

Next I surveyed more than seven hundred junior high school students in three Oklahoma cities to find out what they already knew about the Vietnam War and what questions they were most interested in having answered. The survey instrument was simple. It was a sheet of paper. On one side students were asked to write five to ten statements that they knew were true about the war, and on the other side they were to write five to ten questions they would like to have answered.

I found that although the students were very interested in the war, they knew little about it and were concerned about their lack of knowledge. The papers returned to me included the following statements: "I need to become more educated on that subject." "No one has ever taught me about the Vietnam War." "They don't teach about that war in school. All I know about the Vietnam War has come out of movies." "It might be kind of a shame, but I don't know anything about the Vietnam War." "How come they don't teach more about the war in school?" "Is anyone else as dumb about this as I am?"

Students have made it clear to me that they see this as the war no one wants to talk about. They seem to be saying that they know the war is the skeleton in America's family closet, and that they think they are now old enough to be let in on the secret.

The tremendous interest in this subject among students is something that teachers should capitalize on. As a junior high school teacher my job is often divided into two parts. Before I can start teaching about a subject, I frequently have to find a way to arouse my students' interest. With the Vietnam War the work is half done. The students are already interested. Their knowledge, though, is limited.

Students' statements of what they knew about the war included the following: "The war was fought to save U.S. prisoners from Vietnam." "It was really us against ourselves." "I know that Americans always fought each other in their camps." "We dropped a bomb on Hiroshima." "We should not have gotten involved in it because there are still millions of our men over there." "It took place in the Philippines." "I know that it was as bad as I can only dream."

The most common responses were:

1. Many Americans were killed.
2. It took place in Vietnam.

3. The United States lost.
4. American POWs are still being held.
5. It took place in the 1960s and 1970s.

The questions I received were often interesting, too. Among them were: "If they're having a war why are little kids there?" "Are some men still alive that fought in it?" "Did the U.S. fight in the war?" "Did they have automobiles back then?" "How many heroes were there?" "How many people tried to prevent that war?" "What were all of the names of the people who served in the Vietnam War, if you know?"

The five questions asked most often were:
1. What was the cause?
2. When was the war?
3. How many Americans were killed?
4. What countries fought in the war?
5. Who won?

The survey gave me a pretty good idea of what students knew and wanted to know about the war, but I realized I would still need help deciding what they should be taught about the war.

I decided to write letters to people who had been involved in some way with the war. I went through a dozen books on the war and wrote down every name that was in the bibliographies or indexes. I then went to *Who's Who In America, Current Biography,* and a few other sources to find out which of the people on my master list were still alive and prominent enough to have a current address listed. I wrote to a broad group of people, including decision makers who had been in the government during the war, prominent journalists, authors of books on the subject, leading voices in opposition to the war, and public figures in America today. The letter I sent to each person asked this question: "What do you think are the most important things for today's junior high students to understand about the Vietnam War?" I wrote each letter by hand, hoping that the personal touch might encourage more people to consider my request.

The replies started coming in immediately. Throughout the summer of 1987, I was receiving letters almost daily. As our school year began in August, I was still receiving letters. I decided to begin my American history course that year with a discussion of the Vietnam War and the 1960s. Although I will always have the letters to use in my classes, I will never again be able to capture the excitement of those two weeks in August. Each day I would excuse myself from my class just long enough to go to my mailbox in the administrative office of the junior high. I would then return with the day's mail, open the letters in front of the class, and say, "Okay, let's see what Barry Goldwater has to say," or, "Here's what Tom Hayden wants you to know."

My collection of letters soon developed into something I thought might be of national interest. I had repeatedly told my students that, while the letters were all addressed to me, the letter writers were actually speaking to them. So I knew the letters were something that should be shared with everyone.

I wrote to Richard Snow, managing editor of *American Heritage* magazine, and a few months later a selection of the letters appeared as the cover article in the May, 1988, issue.

After the magazine article appeared, I was able to obtain letters answering my question from an even wider array of interested people, including combat veterans and mothers who had lost sons in the war. From the very beginning of this project, virtually everyone took great care in answering my question, and I am grateful to all who were willing to help me gain a better understanding of the war so that I could do a better job of teaching about it.

What Should We Tell Our
Children About Vietnam?

Michael Arlen

Writer; author of *Living Room War* and *An American Verdict*

First of all, I hope that your students will learn about history, the expanse of history—not all of it right away!—but more than many of their peers and predecessors seem to have learned. And not just American history! And not try to understand it all at once, because to understand often means to define, often to define too tightly, and if the passage of history teaches us anything, I suspect it teaches that history—that is, our perception of past events—is continually changing and evolving.

What I have told my own children is that there are two purposes to education. One is to be able to share in a cultural pool—to be aware of the reference points (at least the most significant ones) that our society has marched by in its long journey out of the mud. The other is to be able to think independently—that is, to be able to tell the difference between first-rate and second- or third- rate information, because information of itself has no intrinsic value, and not being able to tell the difference between accurate and inaccurate information can be dangerous.

For example, it's interesting to consider that the Vietnam War—contrary to what many people think—was a war that was entered into with probably more discussion and debate at the top levels of government than any other war we have engaged in. That doesn't make it good or right or worth having entered. But it might make one a bit more modest in the stance one takes from hindsight—modesty in the face of history being a not ignoble demeanor in my opinion. If good and serious and generally decent people could make such mistakes, what are we doing (what seriousness, for instance, are we bringing to our monitoring of officials?) to prevent such mistakes being made in the future?

For example, people often remark that television affected

3

the outcome of the war by making the home audience so conscious of the horrors of war that large segments of the populace marched in the streets to protest it. It's true that many people protested the war on the home front, for many diverse reasons, some based on a concern for war or for Vietnam, others for more personal or self-serving reasons. But television almost never, not until the final days of the war, showed anyone the horrors of war. Television news, in fact, refused to show American troops dying until the final days, and certainly there was none of that bloody stuff that is now so much admired for its reality in movies such as *Platoon*.

My own opinion about television and Vietnam is that its effects were contradictory. To some extent television showed us war (though not its horrors) and turned the audience against it. To some extent, in the safe banality of its coverage (especially in the early years), television banalized war and made it seem okay, manageable, winnable.

In the end what I urge on your students is to live their lives in such a way that they not be burdened by what strikes me as democracy's most notable drawback—namely, the seeming tendency of democratic peoples to be surprised by life. For if there is one false note in much of the distress and pain that have been expressed about Vietnam, it is this element of surprise, this "Why me?" *Why me?* is not a tragic cry, alas. Death or injury is awful, terrible. Death or injury in a needless event is even worse. But *Why me?* or *How did I get here?* doesn't help anything. *Why me?* simply means one hasn't been watching the road, as people for the most part are not watching the road now. In the great tragedies of bygone times there is no *Why me?* There are men (and sometimes women) in terrible situations, sometimes railing at the gods, or at God. These are men and women caught up in self-awareness (which is what makes Greek tragedy the powerful thing it is). But to be without self-awareness, to be without history, is to be a child in ignorance, which may be charming or at least tolerable in a very young person but is dangerous and wasteful in a man or a woman.

Richard Armitage

Naval Operations Coordinator, Defense Attaché Office, Saigon, Vietnam, 1973–75; Assistant Secretary of Defense, 1983–

In my view there are three main points to understand about our involvement in the Vietnam War:

First, the U.S. government was unwilling or, perhaps, unable to articulate effectively goals and objectives for our involvement in Vietnam, thus failing to mobilize public support for this sacrifice. Second, the government failed to realize that *Dau Tranh* (Vietnamese for "struggle") had both military and political applications and that the Vietnamese Communists gave equal weight to both sides of the equation. Third, once committed to sacrifice, we did not fight to win, because of political constraints. We entered negotiations with the Communists without understanding that in their view negotiation means "What is mine is mine and what is yours we will talk about." To us, compromise is an honorable and reasonable process. To Communists, compromise is weakness. The Communists realize that one cannot win at the bargaining table that which was lost in the war, but that one could lose at the table that which has been achieved.

The three foregoing points, however, do not suggest that the blood and treasure sacrificed by the United States and, more particularly, U.S. servicemen and women in Vietnam was for naught. Arguably, the non-Communist nations of Asia have thrived, and this has been so because of the time bought for them by the sacrifice of our nation and our people. One of the great ironies of the Indochina conflict is that the nations that won the war have lost the peace.

I believe that young Americans have to realize that foreign policy involves difficult choices, and that crisp, clean answers to difficult questions are almost impossible to obtain. Hence a steady, consistent approach to world problems, based on sound moral judgments, serves us best. But once set upon a policy course, our system demands that we develop sufficient understanding among our populace to support our actions. Patience is not a well-known attribute of democracy; thus a consistent and credible rationale for our actions must be presented to enable the government to continue its course.

Heidi (Bud) Atanian

Crew Chief, 282nd Assault Helicopter Company (Black Cat), Hue Section, 1967–68

The thing about the war that I would most like for everybody to understand is who the kids fighting it were. You'll note I used the term *kids.* It's not a put-down but simply a fact. Most of us were kids. Picture if you will a guy two or three years older than you, if you're a junior high school student. He graduates from high school and then is either drafted or enlists in the military. Eight to ten weeks of basic training pass quickly. Then he gets another five to ten weeks of advanced individual training. I enlisted in the army in August, 1966. By January, 1967, I was on my way to Southeast Asia to fight a war. Think about that for a moment—the transition experienced by these kids. A few short months ago they were chasing girls, getting drunk on Friday night, and worried about school, work, or their cars. Then they find themselves in a rice paddy or a helicopter fighting a war.

Who were these kids? Most were eighteen to twenty years old. Most were not high school graduates; many were draftees; minorities appeared to be heavily represented. Why were they there? Well, I can truly speak only for myself. I graduated from high school and was all set to go to college, but my country was at war. I think I acted much the same way a kid during World War II would have acted. My country was at war, so my patriotic duty was to go and fight. Boy does that sound pie in the sky, but it's the truth. I and many others were brought up to think that way, and I truly hope it's still that way today.

What was the tour of duty like? Well, for each individual the experience was different. The experience for me was profound, and I'm sure it changed my life. The friendships that developed will last a life time. A good example of that was last year's Black Cat reunion. Most of us had not seen or spoken to each other in twenty years, but it took only a few seconds to reestablish the bonds.

My tour was eighteen months. Many days were dull with routine daily duties. Many days were exciting with the rush or high of combat. Many days were rewarding with the excitement of evacuating a wounded soldier and knowing the actions taken by you and your crew would send that soldier home to his family alive rather than in a box. Many days were sad with the death of a friend.

Coming home was perhaps the strangest experience. One day I was in a war zone; the next I was in the states. There was no welcome home like there had been after other wars. We were given instructions and sent home in a matter of hours. You go to the airport for a flight home, and people look at you funny. No one seems to care. Your family greets you, and they are glad you're home, but even they can't understand what you've been through. To this day I feel truly meaningful conversations on the war can take place only between veterans.

What should you understand? Understand the folks that went and fought that war. We were not drug-crazed baby killers. We were kids trying to cope and survive in a difficult situation. We loved our country and were glad to serve. To this day we feel we could have and should have won that war, and we say never again send us to fight a war we are not 100 percent committed to win. We are kids who most likely would do it all again.

Al Auster

Coauthor of *How the War Was Remembered: Hollywood and Vietnam*

I believe that the important things for junior high school students to understand about the Vietnam War are the following:

1. The war was fought from misconceptions about the nature of nationalism and communism—presuming that communism was monolithic, and that nationalism could somehow be defeated by pure technological superiority.

2. America lost the war because it was not willing or able to make a total war commitment.

3. America could not make that commitment because of the widespread popular opposition to the war.

4. The war undermined some basic shibboleths of American foreign policy—i.e., that the United States was somehow more virtuous than its adversaries.

5. The war changed the nature of American foreign policy or, put another way, created certain restraints, both institutionally and strategically, that American foreign policy could not go beyond. That is, what we refer to as the "Vietnam syndrome" is really built-in restraints on an activist military foreign interventionism.

6. The war was a factor in creating the counterculture of the 1960s, which had a profound effect on the American middle class and its culture.

D. B.

Vietnam veteran

To answer your question, I would say: A warmongering, war-profiteering country sold its poor, disadvantaged, and minorities down the Mekong River while it gave free rides to easy street to everyone who came along with a sob story.

I would also say that we psychopathic, drug-crazed, baby-killing war criminals were left swinging in the wind by an uncaring and unappreciative country that only now is starting to pay us lip service, which does nothing more than add insult to injury.

That's what you should tell your students and your children (if you dare).

Howard Bale

Former member of the Army of the Republic of Vietnam; left Vietnam at the age of twenty-nine

It has been said that in Vietnam the United States ended up fighting an unwinnable war because of the broad popular support for the Viet Cong among the South Vietnamese people and because of the corruption of the South Vietnamese government. The first point is mistaken and unjustified, and the second point is one-sided and unfair. I would like to clarify these obscured points of view:

1. Most South Vietnamese never willingly supported the Viet Cong, but were forced by "the points of bayonets" to help Communist guerillas. In any area, if the people were well-protected, the activities of Communists decreased speedily. Many preju-

diced, immature U.S. soldiers looked at any black-pajama–clad peasant as being a Viet Cong sympathizer. But if you knew the language and culture you would have known that the majority of these "VC" were just honest peasants who did not care about anything except their rice fields.

2. The U.S. government "supplied" South Vietnam not only with war materials but with South Vietnamese leaders as well. If you were a patriot (but not a yes-man) you'd be assassinated. (Remember President Ngo Dinh Diem, who was murdered by U.S.-backed Vietnamese generals in 1963?) But if you followed Washington's orders without questioning them, you'd be left alone (even if you were a corrupt leader, like Nguyen Van Thieu).

So the blame here should absolutely not go to South Vietnam (and keep in mind, the last presidential election in South Vietnam was actually a one-candidate election—so Nguyen Van Thieu absolutely did not represent South Vietnam, but rather he was a war broker of Washington).

3. In his book, *In The Jaws of History*, Bui Diem, a former security adviser to the South Vietnamese government, stated that the first U.S. Marine units that landed at Da Nang did so without the official permission of the South Vietnamese government. The idea of the South Vietnamese government calling the United States for help is a myth.

More than two million South Vietnamese soldiers and civilians sacrificed their lives for freedom. Their view also deserves to be heard, doesn't it?

Robert E. Barrett

Served with the 1st Infantry Division, Vietnam, 1967–68; served with the 3rd Brigade of the 1st Cavalry, Vietnam, 1971–72; Military Aide to President Gerald Ford, 1974–76

I would suggest the following points as being key to the understanding of the Vietnam War:

1. The United States learned for the first time that might doesn't necessarily prevail. In the years ahead, this will become a very positive learning experience for our country in that we must live and survive in the world by our wits as well as by our defenses.

2. The sacrifice of those who served in Vietnam is as noble as the service of those who served in all previous wars. No war ever makes sense to a soldier, but his willingness to serve in a difficult situation is the measure his country demands. Therefore, we should respect the sacrifices of those individuals, because as a contribution to our country's learning, their sacrifice was not wasted.

William T. Bennett

General Secretary, National Vietnam Veterans Coalition

With respect to your letter asking for the most important things to understand about Vietnam, we do not have any good answers. There are probably as many answers as there are people.

One can validly argue, at one extreme, that the war was just and noble and would have been won but for the "stab in the back." One can validly argue, at the other extreme, that the war was immoral (or at least stupid) and that defeat was near inevitable. There are a host of reputable intermediate viewpoints. Every other question involving the war is subject to similar diversity of viewpoint.

The only thing that I would personally suggest is that the burden of military service was not equitably distributed among socioeconomic classes. Thus, the generational leadership of our country is now passing, on the one hand, to antiwar activists (many of whom, despite their high-flown rhetoric, came to that position primarily to avoid the interruption of self-indulgence required of military personnel) and, on the other, to tough-minded rhetoricians who kept their draft exemptions carefully in order when the opportunity presented itself to practice what they now preach.

D. M. Boulay

Nurse in Vietnam, 1967–68

I think the most important thing for today's junior high school students to understand about the war fought in Vietnam by the Americans, the Australians, the Koreans, and the New Zealanders in the sixties and early seventies is that it was given a misnomer. It was the perspective of us and our allies to call it "The Vietnam War." The Vietnamese saw it as a civil war—theirs. I wish I had grasped that basic concept when I first went there.

That leads to the second lesson: Our country, specifically, the Congress, which has the constitutional power, never declared that the United States was at war. This was a political decision and begins to provide insight into the intense trauma, debate, and protest that took place.

Third, war is war, with or without a capital W, and when we waged it half a world away, we assumed many responsibilities we have not fulfilled. We wasted a countryside, harmed the people, and helped to forever change an entire culture, but we have not begun to make restitution, because it is still a question of politics that seems too volatile to handle, even twenty years later.

It would seem the ultimate lesson is that if we, as a country, need or want to wage war, it must be a decision of the people, and not just of a few leaders. Also we must, if we choose to wage war, accept the full measure of our responsibilities. We must be accountable to those we willingly or negligently harm and disrupt; we must rise above politics and assert our humaneness. We must do what is right.

M. Chuck Bowman

Two-tour Vietnam veteran, Marines, 1964–66

I think our youth should be taught the lesson of Vietnam in a comparative context, as it relates to our own American Revolution and its success. That revolution probably would have been doomed to the might of England had not the French and others, for self-serving reasons, assisted the colonies.

So also the struggle by the South Vietnamese to resist communism was doomed when the politicians of this country couldn't find the moral courage, or even selfish reasons, to support them.

When our cowardly, self-serving, reelection-at-any-cost Congress capitulated to the equally cowardly, self-serving antiwar protests, Vietnam, Cambodia, and Laos became the sacrificial lambs on the altar of political expediency.

Unlike the Jane Fondas and Tom Haydens, I feel a moral obligation to assist the efforts of any people of this earth to resist Communist domination.

Vietnam is gone, as are Cambodia and Laos. Every year the false promise of Communist equality, at the sacrifice of freedom, devours even more of the world around us like a cancer, never relinquishing what it acquires.

The lesson of Vietnam? It should have been learned from the Nazis and every other terrorist government that has ever existed. Stated simply and eloquently, by someone whose name escapes me, it can be paraphrased this way:

> When they came for my neighbor, I only stood and watched.
> When they came for my other neighbor, I turned away.
> When they came for me, there was none left to help me.

I can only wonder how many generations will pass before there is no one to assist when communism comes for the United States, as it surely will if we continue to turn away. I can be grateful that it probably won't happen in my lifetime, but sad for the probability that it will happen.

Since history has been and will be written by the victors, it is unlikely that my view will be the one that survives in the future.

Peace at any price is a poor god to worship, and, coming from a nation that has sacrificed so much for freedom, one that galls me to no end.

Our forebears cannot but be ashamed at what we are becoming. I am.

Charles L. Boyer

Conscientious objector; Campus Minister at Purdue University, West Lafayette, Indiana, 1964–69

I was a conscientious objector to war who was drafted in June, 1959, immediately after my college graduation. I performed two years of alternative service in Europe, returned to the United States, and completed a master of divinity degree. I then served as a campus minister at Purdue University from 1964–69. While at Purdue, I became closely identified with the antiwar movement and engaged in considerable draft counseling.

Purdue University in the 1960s was renowned for its engineering and agriculture schools. In 1964, when I arrived on campus, Purdue was a "hotbed of student *rest*." Little was happening. There was a small chapter of Students for a Democratic Society (SDS). Nearly all SDS members came from large urban areas, especially Chicago and cities on both the East and West coasts. Advisers and concerned faculty were difficult to find. A few professors were about the only people willing to challenge the war openly.

During my five years at Purdue things changed radically. From 1964–66 I was the only campus minister willing to participate in open, antiwar protests on campus. From 1967–69 I never was asked to be an antiwar speaker or religious symbol, because Roman Catholic, United Methodist, United Church of Christ, and many other large denominations had campus clergy denouncing the war.

In my counseling of students, I dealt with between twenty and twenty-five men who became war resisters. Let me share only one of those stories. Ed (not his real name) was an engineering student from Chicago. His mother was an American Jew and his father a Korean Methodist. He was raised as a Jew but had a good knowledge of Christianity.

His opposition to the war was primarily political. He believed the United States was invading Vietnam to benefit "corporate America," as he called it. Religious beliefs were intertwined with his political persuasions, but Ed was not a pacifist and did not fit the Selective Service's criteria of "being opposed to *all* wars." However, Ed was convinced he could not fight in Vietnam and decided to claim conscientious objection to war, hoping that he might perform alternative service in lieu of entering the armed forces.

When Ed's draft board in Chicago received his claim of conscientious objection, they called him in for a hearing. Ed asked me to accompany him to that hearing for moral support and in the hope that I might be allowed to speak on his behalf. The hearing was held six months before Ed was due to graduate.

The draft board hearing was similar to many I have attended over the years. The draft board members had not studied the file ahead of time. They were reading Ed's statements and the testimony of witnesses during the hearing. My presence was acknowledged, but I was not allowed to present testimony. At the end of the hearing the board announced that they unanimously rejected the claim of conscientious objection. Ed was devastated.

What happened to Ed happened to many other young men during the 1960s and up to 1973. They decided to forgo any further appeals and fled the United States. Within ten days after his graduation, Ed was in Canada. His fiancée joined him a year later and they married and established a home there. Ed did not accept any offers of amnesty, and he and his family are now Canadian citizens. His wife returns frequently to the United States. To my knowledge, Ed has never set foot on U.S. soil since he fled in 1968.

Peter Braestrup

Combat correspondent, *New York Times*, Saigon, 1966–68; *Washington Post* Bureau Chief, Saigon, 1968–69; now Editor of *The Wilson Quarterly*

I suggest that there are five things that a junior high school student should understand about the Vietnam War:

1. The war was fought for a noble cause—to defend South Vietnam from a Communist takeover. Events confirmed that a Communist takeover brought great harm to the Vietnamese people; more than a million fled.

2. Presidents Kennedy, Johnson, and Nixon tried to fight the war "on the cheap." They did not ask for Congressional declaration of war; they did not mobilize the country behind the war; they did not develop a long-term strategy for winning

the war; Lyndon Johnson did not face the issue of whether the defense of South Vietnam, and all the costs it entailed, was vital to America's security.

3. American troops, at least until President Nixon began troop withdrawals in 1969, fought as well as (or better than) their elders in World War II or Korea. They were neither victims nor psychopaths (as portrayed in the movie *Platoon*). They were probably better disciplined than their elders; less damage and fewer civilian casualties were inflicted on the South Vietnamese than on the Koreans during the Korean War.

4. The South Vietnamese ally was caught up in a civil war—abetted by outsiders from North Vietnam. The South was historically less united than the North; the South Vietnamese officer corps was the only relatively coherent national organization, hence its members were embroiled in politics. There was no southern counterpart to the extraordinarily well-organized, battle-tested Communist party organization run from Hanoi. Even so, no South Vietnamese army unit ever deserted to the foe. South Vietnamese died in battle in far larger numbers than did the Americans. Some South Vietnamese units, e.g., the Marines and the Airborne, were superb; others were badly led and badly trained. South Vietnam suffered from mediocre political leadership. Yet, in peacetime, South Vietnam would have been as prosperous as Taiwan or Singapore. It was outmatched by the North in a war for survival.

5. Geography and political constraints made an allied victory impossible under the ground rules of 1965–73. Hanoi was able to use Laos and Cambodia freely to reinforce the southern battlefield, always protected by U.S. self-constraints. It was an *Indochina* war, as seen from Hanoi if not from Washington. U.S. forces were not allowed to block the Ho Chi Minh Trail in Laos and Cambodia. As long as the trail was open, the war could not be won, and peace could not come to the South. The trail gave Hanoi the strategic initiative: the North Vietnamese could choose whether to fight or fall back to the "sanctuaries." As the United States set it up, the North Vietnamese simply could outlast us in a contest of wills.

Rodger M. Brodin

Vietnam veteran; sculptor of proposed Vietnam Women's Memorial

It is sad that so many of the young people in our country (including college students) have little or no knowledge of the war in Vietnam.

If I were to write a book on the war, I would not isolate the period 1961 to 1975. The history weaves in and out from the end of World War II to today.

I would trace the politics involved. After World War II the British were "assigned" to secure Southeast Asia. They armed Japanese troops, removed Ho Chi Minh (our ally), and reestablished the French colony of French Indochina. Ho Chi Minh finally kicked the French out. We were involved before the Korean War. President Eisenhower first put American troops in Vietnam in 1958, then President Kennedy installed a Catholic president in that Buddhist country.

I would also talk about the limits we placed on ourselves and the stupid tactics of taking, retreating, and retaking key terrain; the politics, the lies, the misrepresented intelligence, etc. Our country started a new, stupid kind of warfare in Korea, which was perfected in Vietnam.

I would bring up the costs of the war: in dollars, in lives lost during the war, in lives lost since the war due to suicide, in drug and alcohol problems, and in broken homes.

I would point out the over two thousand MIA/POWs and our country's concern to liberate hostages from Iran, Syria, Beirut, and elsewhere, while turning our backs on our brothers in Nam.

I would let people know that women served, as they have in all our wars, and that we are able to talk to friends today who wouldn't be here without their sacrifice.

Malcolm W. Browne

Chief Indochina correspondent, Associated Press, 1961–65; Saigon correspondent, ABC, 1965–66

Your question is about as tough as a question can be, and I certainly don't pretend to know the answer. Put another way, how could you explain to an English or Russian kid living in 1860 what the Crimean War had been all about? A century from now, will anyone remember Vietnam at all, or was it just a footnote to the twentieth century?

Maybe there are a couple of ways to look at it.

One is to suppose that there were two sets of good guys, one led by John F. Kennedy and the other by Ho Chi Minh, who were equally convinced that the other side was the bad guy. After the loss of nearly two million lives and economic damage on both sides, we decided to call it a draw.

We can also look at it as a local test between Soviet expansionism and American resistance to the Soviets. For now, with Hanoi as a loyal Moscow ally and with Soviet warships based at Cam Ranh Bay, it certainly looks like a Soviet victory. But time has a way of changing such things. In 1939 the Fascists gained a clear-cut victory in Spain over the combined forces of the Communists and Democrats. Opposition to the Falange was wiped out, and as long as Francisco Franco lived, Spain remained a Fascist dictatorship. Who could have guessed that four decades after Franco's smashing victory, a peaceful and almost uneventful transition would bring to Spain a liberal political democracy in which dissent and freedom of choice are vigorously encouraged?

Maybe the lesson of Vietnam was this: If you really want to win a war, you're best off fighting it on your own, with as little help from outside as possible. I watched South Vietnamese fighting spirit evaporate in inverse proportion to the level of U.S. aid, combat assistance, and advice that was poured in. It's just possible that Saigon would have waged a better war if we had

19

simply stayed out. In the early 1960s it cost one of the Trung Lap rangers about thirteen cents to kill a guerrilla. When we began using Guam-based B-52s for that job, the cost rose to about $137,000 for every guerrilla killed. The Saigon troops stood back and laughed at us until they realized they were laughing at their own doom, and then it was too late. Fed up, the United States pulled out, and the roof caved in.

Vietnam was like the Battle of the Somme in 1916: a conflict in which a lot of fine people on both sides were killed in vain. Like the Somme, Vietnam had no appreciable effect on history, except to remind survivors that war is a tragic business never to be undertaken lightly. For a junior high student (or anyone else), I think the best prescription is to study history, history, and more history. As someone else said, those who don't know history are doomed to repeat it.

Frances Shea Buckley

Operating room supervisor, USS *Repose*, Vietnam, 1968–69; Rear Admiral, U.S. Navy, retired

It is difficult for me to answer your question, given my perspective of the war. I served aboard a hospital ship, 1968–69, as an operating room nurse. My job was to provide care for the seriously wounded—and we had so many. I think I would want junior high school students to understand that, given the intensity of the war and magnitude of responsibility in caring for casualties, few of us had the time or energy to philosophize about the morality of the war. That was left to others in the states.

I'd want them to know that all the casualties were brave, often more concerned about the status of their "buddy" than for themselves. Whenever they found wounded Vietnamese, particularly children, they sent them to us for treatment, despite the risk to themselves. Sometimes these Vietnamese were Viet Cong or North Vietnamese Army members.

Those who served in Vietnam were special men and women who, in spite of the failure of their country to support them, did the best they could because they believed that their country would not ask them to do what was not right. I'd want them to know that the Vietnam veteran has nothing for which he or she needs to apologize.

Finally, they should understand that no one hates war as much as the warriors. There is no glory.

McGeorge Bundy

Special Assistant to the President for National Security, 1961–66

I would put first the very hard problem of deciding how far and how long to support an ally. I believe, in retrospect, that we should have limited both the time and extent of our commitment to South Vietnam more than we did, but that was a choice that each president rejected, for powerful reasons. Since absolute answers will be wrong—the United States cannot support every friend everywhere with all its strength and, conversely, it cannot abandon every threatened friend—this problem of choice is inescapable, and it can be extraordinarily difficult—as indeed it was in Vietnam.

George Bush

U.S. Ambassador to the United Nations, 1971–72; Director, CIA, 1976–77; Vice-President of the United States, 1981–89; President of the United States, 1989–

I believe the final view of our success and/or failure in Vietnam will not be established for some time. However, several lessons from our involvement in Vietnam come to mind. They are:

—We must ensure that any major foreign policy commitment has the full support and understanding of the American people, for it is through their sons and daughters and their tax dollars that our power and influence are projected. Without such support, a protracted U.S. involvement cannot succeed.

—The United States must have a clear understanding of the historical processes at work. In Vietnam, we misjudged China's role in the war. The United States viewed the Vietnam War as the first step in China's drive to expand its influence throughout Southeast Asia, forgetting the long history of fighting between China and Vietnam over a variety of issues. In fact, the Vietnam War was fundamentally a continuation of a centuries-old fight among various Vietnamese regional factions, and Chinese-Vietnamese hostility reemerged soon after our withdrawal.

—The United States entered the Vietnam War viewing it as another Korea. In fact, the causes for the war, the topography, and the methods used by the enemy were very different, and these differences were not recognized early enough by the United States.

—The United States essentially fought the war for the South Vietnamese. In future conflicts of this type, every effort must be made to encourage the beleaguered people of a country to fight for their own survival, as is being done in Afghanistan and Nicaragua.

Our participation in Vietnam was right, albeit poorly conducted. With the withdrawal of U.S. forces and the collapse of South Vietnam, we have witnessed the mass exodus of the boat people, and we have seen Vietnam's economy deteriorate to a

22

point where it is the poorest major nation in the world today. We fought to spare the South Vietnamese the inevitable consequence of economic failure inherent in a Marxist dictatorship as well as to protect their right of independence and right to self-determination. Our loss was their loss.

However, other nations of Southeast Asia, those that formed the Association of Southeast Asian Nations (ASEAN) alliance, were given the time needed to become stronger. Prime Minister Lee Kwan Yew of Singapore said it best when he stated that the U.S. effort in Vietnam gave ASEAN the time necessary to become economically self-sufficient.

Richard Cameron

Teacher of English literature; has spent most of his teaching years in universities in Southeast Asia

I believe the single most important lesson to be learned from the Vietnam War is that the United States, or any other nation, does not have the legal or moral right to intervene in the affairs of another nation and impose its own vision of order by force against the wishes of that nation's people. I believe it is imperative that our students be given the opportunity at least to discuss *the possibility* that our country was guilty of an act of aggression in Vietnam. I recognize the difficulty of communicating such an idea to students of a very young age; one does not wish to undermine their sense of hope. Nonetheless, it is a matter of clear historical record that our leaders were quite aware that the majority of the Vietnamese supported their own leaders, who had led them to victory over the French. And despite the very real divisions within Vietnamese society as the war progressed, we ourselves were the unwanted intruders, and by the end of our stay we had become a feared and hated presence. To have intervened in such circumstances was to have committed far more than a "mistake." It was to involve ourselves in a grievously immoral and unjust conflict with tragic and ruinous consequences for the peoples of Indochina.

Given the ideology of the times, I do not doubt that many of the American soldiers directly involved in the war initially participated with good intentions. However, it is also a matter of clear historical record that nation-states and the powerful interests that operate within them have a pressing need to rationalize and idealize their most questionable and self-serving actions in terms of lofty and disinterested motives and that these idealized motives are then internalized by the general population. For wherever human nature is found, motives are always mixed, and one cannot escape the universal human need to sacralize the intentions of one's nation. It is one of the great defenses we possess against the fear of our own mortality, to associate ourselves with a concrete, historical power that we believe to be incapable of serious moral fault and that we endow with near transcendent qualities. In this way powerful economic and political interests combine with psychological and religious needs to create a matrix of profound illusion. And all of us are to some extent affected and our perceptions of the world subtly altered.

I believe that many of us Americans during the Indochina conflict were both victims and perpetuators of an ideology and foreign policy that were essentially self-serving. Following the conclusion of the Second World War, we believed in our "mandate" to create a certain economic and political order for the world, and we believed in our moral right to impose this vision upon the peoples of Vietnam and Indochina. We believed that what was good for us would also be good for them, and we blinded ourselves both to the unique characteristics of the nationalist movements we were opposing as well as to the ruinous consequences of our actions, because to see clearly would have contradicted our belief in the purity of our intentions. Yet in this regard, it is well to recall the dictum of Pascal that evil is never so perfectly achieved as when it is done with good will and purity of heart.

Yet how difficult it is to convey these ideas in the America of today, with the spirit of revisionism that is sweeping the nation. It seems we are beset by a fundamental unwillingness to see. And yet to heal the sickness at our nation's heart, I believe that we must accept the painful truth that our cause was unjust because we were not wanted, no matter what crimes the Communist insurgents themselves may have committed. And we must accept the reality that whatever the intentions of individual Americans in the field, the foreign policy that motivated our cause was neither moral nor unselfish. As events in Central America today are making only too plain, we are a nation deeply in need of healing, and this healing can be achieved only by giving the truth the honor and respect it fully deserves.

Philip Caputo

Vietnam veteran; foreign correspondent for *Chicago Tribune*, 1972–77; author of *A Rumor Of War*

The two most important things for today's junior high school students to understand about the Vietnam War are:

1. The United States learned in Vietnam that there are limits to its power and that to exceed those limits invites tragic consequences.

2. The American soldiers who fought in the war did so out of a sense of duty to their country, but their country betrayed them by sending them to an unwinnable war.

Jimmy Carter

President of the United States, 1977–81

This war had a devastating impact on the American public, creating a sense of confusion over purpose and a buildup of mistrust in our high government officials. More important, many precious American lives were lost. To honor these brave men and women and all those who willingly answered their nation's call, we must give our solemn pledge to pursue all honorable means to establish a just and lasting peace in the world, that no future generation need suffer in this way again.

Clark Clifford

Special Counsel to the President, 1946–50;
Presidential Adviser, 1967; Secretary of
Defense, 1968–69

My generation of leaders believed in the 1960s that there was a joint understanding between the Soviet Union and Red China to spread the philosophy of communism throughout Southeast Asia, so that they would have no trouble controlling that area of the world. We were conscious of the grievous default on the part of European nations that permitted Adolf Hitler and the Third Reich to gain power and control over most of Europe. We felt that aggression in Southeast Asia had to be stopped at its inception, or it would spread into the Pacific, to the Philippines, and even as far as Australia and New Zealand.

As the war in Vietnam progressed, and as we poured more and more men into the morass of Southeast Asia, it became clear to some of us that the original calculation was erroneous. Our motivations for becoming involved were moral and highly ethical and humane, but the basic reasoning was fallacious. It is clear to me that we should not have sent American troops to fight in this war and that a final decision to withdraw our participation was correct and should not have been delayed so long. It seems clear now that the national security of the United States was not involved in the war in Vietnam and that when this became clear, our decision was right to withdraw.

William Colby

Chief of the Far East Division of the CIA, 1962–68; Executive Director, CIA, 1972–73; Deputy Director of Operations, CIA, 1973; Director, CIA, 1973–76

War is not a simple affair of fighting an enemy. It involves an understanding of who the enemy is and why and how he will fight. It also requires a clear understanding of the attitudes and capabilities of our allies. From these the president must determine our strategy and the tactics for our war effort. And most of all, the president must determine how to keep the American people informed of why and how they must support the war effort, because without that support the war cannot be successfully fought.

In Vietnam we failed to do these things. We insisted for many years in fighting a soldiers' war, while our enemy was fighting a people's war. We insisted on fighting an American-style war, instead of helping our ally fight a Vietnamese war. And our people were not given a full part in determining whether and how to fight the war. As a result we fought the wrong war for many years. We took the war over from our Vietnamese allies, and our people lost confidence that our government was doing the right thing.

Curiously, we finally learned how to fight the people's war, and did so with success, but too late. When that happened, the enemy turned to a soldiers' war, but the American people by that time refused to support our government in continuing the

27

war, and we withdrew our support of our Vietnamese allies. The result was defeat, and the exodus of over a million Vietnamese from their country to escape the Communist government that won, and the waste of the efforts—and the lives—that America spent there.

When our country faces challenges in the future, we must carefully study our enemies, our allies, and how to fight in the particular time and place where we are challenged. Then we can select the proper strategy and tactics to accomplish our objectives and to keep the necessary confidence and support of the American people. If we study the Vietnam War, we will see why we must do so.

Horace Coleman

Vietnam veteran; poet

I will never forget the two young soldiers I overheard on a bus one day in Saigon. Both had obviously arrived in country recently. Looking out the window, one said to the other, "These people are really dumb. They don't even speak English!" The chauvinism, racism, naïveté, and ignorance that statement expresses say a lot about what happened in Vietnam and why.

I think the study of history—and contemporary history—is extremely important. Our political and military leaders didn't know nearly enough about Vietnamese culture, history, or politics. Nothing has happened to make me think we are any more informed today about geopolitics and the history of nations.

At the earliest possible age, our young people should also be taught our traditions and the good things about our country. They need to understand that we are neither the good guys nor the bad guys but a powerful country playing a difficult role in the world. We were, and are, sometimes correct and sometimes wrong. We must learn from the past and anticipate the future. Before, during, and after Vietnam I learned that:

—A country is entitled to have its own civil war (with referees).

—You should address and assess the real, current situation—not the last one you were in or the one you hope to find.

—A nation's domestic problems travel overseas in its soldiers' rucksacks.

—A one-year tour is not long enough to learn your job in a combat zone, become effective, and train your replacement.

—America's procurement system does not necessarily produce the finest, best-suited, most reliable, and most cost-effective weapons systems.

—Americans were basically indifferent to the war, and those who fought it, perhaps for three reasons: (1) it was too far away to matter; (2) they couldn't see the immediate threat; (3) their loved ones were not involved.

—It is better to be a soldier than a civilian in a war zone.

—Democracy is *not* the best form of government for all people at all times.

—Except for dedicated Marxists/politicians, communism is the choice of desperate people. Give them better alternatives.

—Fire control was *very* weak. People bombed, shelled, and shot too fast and too often.

—Forces with sound political and historical grounds are better motivated.

—Given equally bad situations, America is more likely to act against a left-wing than a right-wing government.

—Governments usually don't tell their citizens the real reason(s) for fighting.

—Guys on your side can be just as vicious as the enemy.

—If it's not worth your daughter's life, it's not worth my son's.

—Moral cowardice—the inability to say, "This is not working"—may have been our greatest error.

—Neither John Wayne nor Ronald Reagan ever fought a war.
—Majorities may rule, but they're not always right.
—Men fight because of indoctrination, pride, and not wanting to let the other guys down.
—Mistreating your veterans is not a good idea. It'll be harder to coax their sons into the next war.
—Most people will get out of a dirty job if they can.
—Our attitudes and behavior toward our allies undermined our military/political objectives. Far too often we treated them like "niggers" in their own country.
—Our overwhelming air supremacy prevented even higher casualties.
—People who think they are too valuable to be risked in combat are usually wrong.
—That saying really goes, "My country right or wrong. When right to keep her right. When wrong to set her right."
—The biggest "hawks" are usually found farthest from the battle.
—The government, the country, and the people are *not* one and the same.
—The greater the sacrifice, the fewer the patriots.
—The military is less racist than the general population.
—The only rights you have are those you can defend.
—The way other people do things makes perfectly good sense to them.
—There are worse things than dying.
—Those who actually fight a war usually get the least out of it.
—Trying hard doesn't mean you'll win.
—Vietnam was under Chinese control for nine hundred years without wiping out all resistance. During a weak dynasty, the Vietnamese revolted. We should have paid attention to that.
—War *is* good for business—if you're in the right business.
—War is usually boring, sometimes exciting, often deadly, never glamorous.
—We care more for good working relationships with govern-

ments than for good will with their citizens. Governments change; the people choose them (if they can).

—Working-class white ethnics, blue-collar whites, and racial minorities took the brunt of Vietnam.

—You can't trust your government. You have to fight it for your rights and benefits.

—You never really get over it.

Harvey Cox

Professor of Divinity, Harvard University, 1970–

During the course of the war I became increasingly convinced that it was a mistake and that the courage and bravery of the young men and women who were sent there was being utilized for purposes not in keeping with the best values of American society. I became an opponent of the war and participated in many of the actions and demonstrations that the opposition organized.

It is important, however, for your students to realize that many of us who opposed the war felt a deep kinship with and admiration for people like yourself who were actually fighting the war. In fact, I remember one returning veteran who told me that in many ways he felt closer to those who had opposed the war than to people who "didn't give a damn." At least the soldiers who fought the war and those of us who opposed it had strong feelings about it and were willing to engage in sacrificial activities to various degrees to make our convictions clear.

I have been enormously impressed by the two visits I have made to the Vietnam Memorial, in Washington, D.C. One of the things that makes it so successful is that as the memory of the war recedes, the monument keeps vivid the price paid by those who died. I have also noticed that both those who opposed the war and those who favored it are equally impressed by the monument and by the register of names of those who lost their lives during it.

The Vietnam War was a period of great division in our country, but I think it is beginning to be remembered by those on different sides as something about which we can now come back together.

Mike Dafoe

Team leader, Vietnam Veterans Center, Sioux Falls, South Dakota

The legacy of the Vietnam War is an opportunity for Americans to look at themselves differently in light of what is going on in the rest of the world. It was a humbling experience for our nation. It's important for veterans of all wars to portray a realistic view of what war is about. War is monotonous and boring, with a few moments of intensity. The reality is that a lot of people go to war, and some don't come back. If they do come back, they come back changed.

Phillip Davidson, Jr.

Veteran of World War II, Korea, Vietnam; Chief Intelligence Officer to Generals William Westmoreland and Creighton Abrams, Vietnam; author of *Vietnam At War: The History, 1946–1975*

First, the Vietnam War was *not* a civil war, nor a South Vietnamese insurgency. The Geneva Accords of 1954 established two separate, independent countries, each exercising all the functions of sovereignty. Only in the late fifties and early sixties could the conflict in South Vietnam be called an insurgency. During that relatively short period the Viet Cong, composed largely of "regrouped"

Communist southerners from North Vietnam, did the fighting. Even then the Viet Cong were completely controlled by the North Vietnamese. From 1964, when the first North Vietnamese Army (NVA) regular army units entered South Vietnam, until 1975, the war was an outright invasion of South Vietnam by North Vietnam.

Second, our motives for helping the South Vietnamese were moral. We wanted to prevent a small democracy from being subjugated by a Communist state by force of arms. The United States wanted no territory in Vietnam, none of its scarce natural resources, and no military bases there.

Third, the United States lost the Vietnam War. Our national mission was best expressed in a government memorandum dated March 17, 1964, which stated that our national objective was "to preserve South Vietnam as an independent, non-Communist state." Obviously, we didn't do that.

Fourth, American forces won every battle in, over, and around Vietnam. Our forces there conducted themselves not only with great military effectiveness but, by and large, honorably and decently.

Fifth, how could the United States win every battle in Vietnam and yet lose the war? The answer—we didn't understand the kind of enemy we were trying to defeat. We fought the kind of war the enemy wanted us to fight, allowing him to take advantage of our weaknesses (e.g., shaky support at home), while we failed to use our strengths against his weaknesses. We should have declared war against North Vietnam in 1964 and used our overwhelming military strength to bring the war to a speedy and satisfactory conclusion. To have done so would have been more humane and less costly than the drawn-out, limited war we fought and lost.

Chuck Dean

Vietnam veteran; Executive Director, Point Man International; author of *Nam Vet*

I believe that the students of America understanding fully why we could not gain the victory we sought in Southeast Asia will be a major determining factor in this country's future decision-making regarding foreign wars. Students should be taught a complete analysis of the demoralizing DEROS (Date Eligible to Return from Overseas) system, in which a one-year tour gave individual soldiers the sole purpose of serving a sentence instead of winning a war.

John Gunther Dean

Assistant Economic Commissioner, Saigon, 1953–56; Political Officer, Laos, 1956–58; Regional Director, Civil Operations and Revolutionary Development Support (CORDS), Central Vietnam, 1970–72; Deputy Chief of Mission, American Embassy, Laos, 1972–74; Ambassador to Cambodia, 1974–75

I believe the youth of today must realize that the foreign policy of our government must enjoy the support of the people of our country. This support is reflected by the views of the elected representatives to our Congress. In short, to be fully effective a foreign policy proposed by the executive branch must be endorsed and fully supported by the people of our country through our elected legislators.

David Dellinger

Antiwar activist; defendant in the "Chicago 8" trial

I think the most important thing for junior high school students to understand about any such question is that every new generation comes along with new insights and a new perspective. Albert Camus once said to "beware all veterans." I think that includes both war veterans and antiwar veterans. Veterans of all kinds have genuine insights that junior high school students should listen to and take into account, but veterans also are scarred by their experiences, experiences in which they invested heavily, both psychologically and physically. In the end, junior high school students must make up their own minds and make decisions and commitments that are true to their own insights and understandings. I am thinking not just about past wars, both overt and covert, but about other controversial questions, such as U.S. activities in Central America, the Persian Gulf, and elsewhere.

Second, it is important to remember what Senator J. William Fulbright, who was chairman of the Senate Foreign Relations Committee during the Vietnam War said ten years later: "The biggest lesson I learned from Vietnam is not to trust government statements. They fix the facts to fit the policy."

Third, it is important to remember that honorable people sincerely differ in their opinions and judgments on such matters. Don't let those differences make you self-righteous or hostile toward those who are thinking and acting differently than you are. As Martin Luther King, Jr. said, we can have opponents on such questions, but we should never treat them as enemies. Today, more and more Vietnam veterans and anti-Vietnam War veterans are finding that they both worked for what they thought at the time was in the best interests of the people of this country and of Vietnam. Together they are trying to prevent new Vietnams in other parts of the world.

Finally, we know now that in 1969 the United States threat-

35

ened to use nuclear bombs in Vietnam but was restrained by the massive demonstrations against the war. Ordinary people who follow their consciences and speak up on such matters can make a difference, even though it may take time before they get enough people to join them to change dangerous government policies. Today we know that a nuclear war could mean the end of all life on the planet, and that little wars can lead to bigger ones, unless the people assert their democratic rights not just by voting but by other nonviolent methods.

Vu Doan

Vietnamese refugee

Reflecting on my own experience as a Vietnamese refugee who fled to this country at the age of sixteen, I would like to suggest a basic lesson for young Americans. In addition to lessons about national interests and the immorality of war, I feel that young Americans should be made aware of the value of freedom in today's tumultuous world. What scarcely is an issue in the aftermath of the Vietnam War is the deliberate destruction of the Vietnamese social tradition and culture by the Communist government, and the total loss of freedom and basic human rights for millions of Vietnamese since the fall of Saigon, in April, 1975.

In late 1975 the new Vietnamese government confiscated and destroyed all books and magazines, closed down all newspapers, and established a central official daily, *Saigon Giai Phong* (Liberated Saigon), in South Vietnam. Since 1975, millions have been rounded up and sent to "reeducation camps," only to be detained there indefinitely. The harsh realities of these camps— made known by the boat people—are that they are a vast prison system in which wardens play little gods with absolute power over their subjects. International human rights groups monitoring Vietnam estimate that seventy thousand prisoners have been executed in these camps, most without trial. Among those being detained are several thousand intellectuals, writers, journalists, Catholic priests and nuns, Buddhist monks, and other religious leaders.

The desperate plight of the boat people is another human tragedy. The United Nations High Commission on Refugees estimates that since 1975, of one and a half million boat people who braved the dangers of high seas and piracy in the Gulf of Thailand, more than half never made it to shore. They knew of the dangers and the slim chances of survival, yet they risked their lives. Today the refugee problem has once again become urgent, since Hong Kong and various countries have decided to close down refugee camps and repatriate people who cannot prove that they are political refugees. I am disheartened to see people risking their lives for freedom, only to be greeted by selfishness and cynicism.

The bleak reality in Vietnam today reminds us that fundamental human rights are being constantly violated by dictatorial regimes around the world. In this country we hold freedom and democracy in utmost reverence. Should we consider these values as being different for people from other countries, who are not as fortunate as we are? I strongly feel that American youth must be taught not to ignore and not to be cynical about these fundamental values and how much they mean to the oppressed people around the world.

For me the lesson from the Vietnam War is that Americans were too impatient to help and too harsh on their judgment of a democracy in its infancy. Granting their good intentions, instead of promoting democratic ideas, Americans imposed their policies and interests on their struggling ally, with little understanding of and consideration for Vietnamese culture and aspirations. Maybe the U.S. policy to contain the spread of communism failed because, while Americans preach freedom and democracy at home, American foreign policymakers see only self-interests and geopolitics. We must not forget that America is still the beacon of democracy and freedom—a valuable heritage to be treasured and defended by all Americans.

Sharon Dodd

Sister of Phillip Sanders, killed in Vietnam, 1970

The Vietnam War was a time in life never to be understood by the families of those who lost their lives. Even after fourteen years have passed, it remains as clear as yesterday.

Having a brother listed as an MIA for two weeks was the most terrifying time of my life. As each day went by, bringing no news, we kept hanging on to a small piece of hope. Then the last report came to our front door. I don't know which was worse—the waiting or the final word. Our lives would never be the same.

If I live to be one hundred years old, the memories of my brother and the horrifying reality of the Vietnam War will always be with me. One request Phil made when he left was to be remembered if he never made it back home. That is the least we can do.

While my brother was in Vietnam, he wrote a poem and sent it home to my mother. He asked her to have it printed in our hometown newspaper to let everyone know what it was like being overseas. The newspaper would not print it when she took it to them nineteen years ago. She has carried it in her purse all this time.

Here is the poem:

> The Fighting Soldier's Life in Viet Nam
>
> Here I am in Viet Nam, fighting
> A cold, cold war,
> Why I am fighting I do not
> Know what for;

I am fighting everyday, and praying
For peace,
I think since it is my life they
Should tell me what I am fighting for
At least;

By my side many men fight and
Die,
And on the wet and bloody ground
They lie;

In Viet Nam there are many many
Men,
All hoping and praying that this
War will end;

They too would like to be at
Home,
With their loved ones they left
All alone;

Over here we are classified as
Men,
But at home we are classified as
Boys again;

Yet we are old enough to
Fight,
But the way they treat us is a
Sight;

We stay out in the cold and
Rain,
And all through the day we are
Constantly in pain;

As we walk through the mud and water
Getting all wet,
A mess our feet are in you can
Bet;

From home we are a long long
Way,
But home I plan to be some
Day.

Yes it is a miserable
Life,
When at home you have a
Wife;

But this is the way a fighting soldier
Has to live in Viet Nam,
Until this war ends between us
And the Viet Cong.

The End

by P.F.C. Phillip D. Sanders

Robert F. Drinan

U.S. Representative from Massachusetts,
92nd–96th Congresses; Professor of Law,
Georgetown University; author of *Vietnam and Armageddon*

When I was a member of the U.S. Congress, I worked diligently to end that terrible conflict.

I do hope that students will learn that the war was immoral and unjust and that, in addition, the United States, in my judgment, has a very strong moral duty to give restitution to the people of South and North Vietnam.

The amount of illegal damage done to the people of Vietnam is simply incredible.

We are now indemnifying American soldiers who were harmed medically by Agent Orange when they were in Vietnam. Why don't we begin to think of giving some restitution to the millions of people in Vietnam who were also hurt by Agent Orange?

Richard Dudman

Washington bureau, *St. Louis Post–Dispatch*, 1954–81; first American reporter to tour Vietnam after the end of the Vietnam War; author of *40 Days with the Enemy*

Here are some of the most important things today's junior high school students should understand about the Vietnam War:

1. The United States has a preoccupation with the menace of communism, deliberately cultivated by politicians, often for their own self-interest, although sometimes out of sincere conviction.

2. This national obsession has blinded the American people and their leaders to many historical developments, notably the Sino-Soviet split and the specific, local causes of many local or regional conflicts. It has led our nation into a number of misguided foreign adventures, including efforts to overturn other governments, including those of Cuba (Bay of Pigs), Guatemala, Chile, Brazil, Iran, China, and Nicaragua.

3. This obsession led directly to a creeping intervention in Vietnam, in the mistaken belief that Ho Chi Minh's revolution was a direct outgrowth of something known as "international communism" and that any such tentacle of this supposedly threatening octopus had to be chopped off wherever it appeared.

4. When government leaders find that a foreign adventure is going sour, they often tell lies, such as the frequent assertion in the course of the Vietnam War that they saw "light at the end of the tunnel." We know from the Pentagon Papers, a secret official history of the war eventually made public, that most of our leaders knew for years that the war was a losing effort that could end only in worsening disaster.

5. When an adventure begins to go sour, our leaders often pretend to concede that the critics have a point but insist that we have already "passed the point of no return." They begin saying this early, seeking to blunt all arguments that they should close down the enterprise and cut their losses.

6. Part of what kept the Vietnam War going so long was a widespread national belief in the old jingoistic slogan, "My

country right or wrong." A better slogan, proposed, as I recall, by a U.S. senator from Missouri, is "My country right or wrong—if right to be kept right, if wrong to be set right."

7. Finally, when criticizing a policy of our own government, one should be wary of assuming that the other side is wise and honest. Some American critics of the Vietnam War fell into the trap of overlooking the faults of the Vietnamese Communists. Among other things, this mistake left the Americans ill-prepared for the stupid action of the Hanoi government, cocky over its victory over the United States, in invading Cambodia in 1979 and setting up its own puppet regime there.

Ted Engelmann

Air Force Sergeant, Vietnam, 1968–69; educator; photojournalist

As a science teacher for seventh and eighth grade at a middle school in Lafayette, Colorado, I learned a lot about what children were interested in when the topic was Vietnam.

Some of the kids would come in after school and ask questions about what life was like in the military: What was it like to get drafted, what was it like to be away from home, and did I ever get hurt? Others asked about their own personal lives: their fathers or stepfathers were Nam vets, and sometimes they behaved in ways the kids didn't understand.

There was also the student who called me late at night, scared, saying there were a lot of police at the house right behind his, and he was afraid something bad had happened. He was unfortunately right. Another Nam vet had put a gun to his head and pulled the trigger. The kid couldn't understand why.

There were also the embarrassing situations I found myself in. During one class I heard the fire siren across the street sound off for the first time. The pitch was just a hair off but still so close to the wail of the base-camp siren at Lai Khe screaming of a Viet Cong ground attack that I flattened myself against the blackboard and immediately headed for the only exit, while thirty wide-eyed seventh graders stared in utter amazement at their weird teacher. Later it was seen as a little joke (I think), and soon talk came around to reactions the kids had seen in other people in response to car backfires and other startling noises.

These children have lived the legacy of Vietnam but don't know what it was all about. Through them, I think we all might breathe a little easier, getting past a few of our own ghosts. I feel there are two areas for junior high school students to consider: themselves and others.

About themselves, I would stress the importance of knowing what their personal values are and how to keep those values when faced with difficult decisions. When today's young people become adults, they will face an increasingly complicated world. They will be called on to use creative problem solving skills and good decision making and critical thinking skills. They will inevitably make humiliating mistakes. Having done that, it's hard to come back and try again, but you must. We learn from mistakes, and it seems that we are all doing the best we know how every second. We're making the best decisions we can. You are here on Earth for a special purpose, and you're doing great. Keep working on it. We usually end up being our own worst critics, so don't push too hard, but keep your values out there and follow your heart, mind, and spirit.

About *other* issues, I think junior high school students should know that Vietnam veterans are people from all walks of life, just like everybody else. We were no more prepared to encounter this trauma called Vietnam than any other generation, and we still feel pain from the experiences each of us had during that time (military *or* civilian).

I get concerned when I hear students (and adults) generalize that all vets were combat vets (for each "combat" vet there were about eight "support" vets) or that any film (*Platoon*, *Good Morning Vietnam*, *Coming Home*, etc.) can tell the whole story of what it was like during that era. There are millions of stories, each true, and each different.

Vietnam veterans are special. So are the veterans of other wars. Our role in war has given us a special wisdom others don't have. We have an obligation to pass this wisdom on to the generations that follow. I hope that wisdom includes compassion for others and the realization that tragedy befalls everyone who is touched by war. The pain is sometimes difficult to get rid of, but as humans we also have a tremendous capacity for healing ourselves from trauma. We can't forget, but we can help ourselves and each other along to a better life in this and future generations.

Dante B. Fascell

U.S. Representative from Florida, 1954–   ; Chairman, Committee on Foreign Affairs, 1984–

It is difficult to answer fully this most thoughtful and provocative question. Let me state at the outset that the "lessons of Vietnam" are ones that should be learned by all age groups, not only junior high school students.

The lessons include: (1) that military force should be employed only in the service of clear-cut political objectives that have a reasonable expectation of being achieved; (2) that the Congress and the American people need fully to understand those objectives and be willing to support them over the long term; and (3) that presidents should not seek to use their considerable authority in carrying out our foreign and national defense policy in a way that ignores, overrides, or supersedes the normal processes of proposals by the executive branch funded by the Congress. Unlawful and unauthorized actions by the president to achieve what he considers to be important objectives are destined to fail when they are eventually revealed.

Irene Faught

Mother of Frank Faught, killed in Vietnam, 1968

I think today's students should be taught the truth about the war, both good and bad. Part of the bad was the way the media handled the news. I think they did a lot to turn people against the boys who went to Vietnam rather than running off to Canada or going to college with no intention of learning while they were there.

Just this week I heard a man who had called into a radio talk show say, "Everybody knows that only the scum went to Vietnam." It hurts to know that some people still think that. My son was not scum! He was a loyal, patriotic man who believed he should serve his country until the point that his country was proved wrong beyond a doubt.

I know that Frank had some doubts about what he was doing. Before he went to Vietnam, he thought about going to Canada. His doubts continued while he was in Vietnam. In one of his letters home he said, "These people don't want us over here."

Then there was the fact that he was supposed to be a security guard in a war situation, but he could not put a bullet in his gun while on guard duty in downtown Saigon.

All in all, it was a very peculiar war, but aren't all wars? I have yet to study about one that I thought was really fair.

Geraldine A. Ferraro

U.S. Representative from New York, 96th–98th Congresses; Vice-Presidential candidate, Democratic party, 1984

I think it is important for today's junior high school students to know that the Vietnam War was, in the minds of most Americans, a mistake. To prevent the same mistake from occurring again, the Congress passed the War Powers Act, which places a responsibility on the Congress to review the actions of a president when troops are in a hostile situation. I truly believe that except for this legislation, President Reagan would have had us more actively participating in the fighting in Nicaragua.

I also think it is equally important to stress that though the war was a mistake, it was the mistake of our government and not of those who were fighting it. Their actions, those of the troops, were those of patriotic Americans who answered their nation's call.

The response of Americans to our returning Vietnam veterans was a disgrace. It is only in the past several years that the dead, with a memorial; the missing, with official governmental investigation; and the sick, with Agent Orange legislation, community outreach programs, etc., are being helped—and all the others, through these less fortunate of their combat brothers, honored. It's very little, very late. Our national anger was misplaced.

Jack Foisie

Los Angeles Times Bureau Chief, Saigon, 1964–66

I think that young Americans ought to be told the unvarnished truth about the American performance in Vietnam—militarily and politically—even though much of it is not pleasant.

There should be mention of how we became involved and why. The why was basically to contain "communism" from spreading south from China into Indochina, much as the United States had done in Europe by assisting Greece after World War II. However, the situation in Vietnam was dissimilar. It was more a war between the haves (landowners) and the have-nots (peasant farmers) with some religious differences mixed in—Buddhists versus Catholics. Our ally, the Saigon government, regardless of its leadership during any particular time, was neither patriotic nor primarily interested in correcting the ills underlying the struggle.

So much for motivation. The initial decision to become involved was made by President Kennedy, but, of course, the buildup of the involvement was primarily that of President Johnson, and the winding down of our participation was a decision made in desperation by President Nixon, and, while necessary, it was not much more than a not very graceful pullout. The truth is: America lost the war in Vietnam. To those who contend that America could have won the conflict by greater commitment had it not been for home-front protesters and a disloyal press in Vietnam, nonsense. Political restraints on our military efforts were a factor, but to have unleashed our forces against the enemy homeland—North Vietnam—would have escalated the conflict to where it might have become World War III.

We could have stayed in Vietnam in a stalemated situation for much longer than we did, but, of course, the growing resentment at home about our presence in Vietnam made that politically impossible.

47

And so a dedicated enemy, willing to accept many casualties and prepared to wait out the impatient Americans, persevered.

Robert Ford

Detachment Commander (Hue Section), 282nd Assault Helicopter Company, Vietnam, 1967–68

From an army helicopter pilot's point of view, there are several things I would want junior high school students to know about the Vietnam War.

I want each of you to know that every warrant-officer pilot, crew chief, and door gunner I flew with was highly motivated, well-trained, humorous, and as courageous as any other soldier the United States produced. We never refused a mission. Discipline was never a problem. There were no drugs. Beer, yes. Teamwork was our strong point. Rank was certainly respected, but strict formality was not required or desired. We were there to serve our country and to perform as was expected.

Like the soldiers in other wars, there were things I missed dearly: my wife (we had been married five months before I left for Vietnam), my family, and walking to the breakfast table and eating a peaceful breakfast that included fresh eggs. Yes—fresh eggs—that was the only food I missed.

There is no way for you to fully understand Vietnam—the feel, the heat, the smell, or the incredible noise—unless you were there. I always wished that my friends and relatives could have come over and flown a fifteen-minute mission with me, and then gone back home.

I've always been bitter that political decisions didn't allow us to win. I was there before, during, and after the Tet offensive of 1968. Unlike what you may have read or heard, we had them close to defeat. With some strategic bombing in North Vietnam and the total disruption of their supply routes, we would have whipped the North Vietnamese Army and the Viet Cong.

Please understand that there is no greater feeling of honor than serving your country. However, if you have to go to war, you will always remember the good men who shared life and death situations with you, the constant humor that kept everyone sane, and the picture of Death—that blank look of Death. I loved those men. *Every day* of your life thereafter you will remember all those things.

J. William Fulbright

U.S. Senator from Arkansas, 1945–74

The principal lesson of the Vietnam War is that the United States should not intervene in other countries with military forces unless that country is a serious threat to our own security. We should not use military force to dictate the political system of another country—especially small countries that wish to have a political system different from ours.

Jere Fullerton, Sr.

Vietnam veteran, U.S. Marines, 1967–68; developed a course on the Vietnam War at Cape Cod Community College, Massachusetts

America had no *vital* interests in Vietnam. By that I mean that we really didn't have any reason to go there in the first place, and it is my opinion that the Gulf of Tonkin incident was provoked by the United States, *not* Vietnam. There is even a question whether anything actually happened at all that night! Second, after troops were committed to the war, we had no strategic objectives. History will support my most important statement of all. Not one single person, including the presidents and congressional leaders of our country, as well as all the top military people in our nation, knew of a plan to win the Vietnam War! That is why our young men found themselves constantly taking territory, only later to give it back to the enemy. Then, several months later, they would have to take the same territory again. It was insane. One hundred and seventy-eight generals and admirals who served in Vietnam were asked the question, "Why was America in Vietnam?" Only 30 percent thought they knew why, and scores were opposed to the way the war was being conducted.

It is important that our young people learn the lessons that Vietnam taught us. The free world looks to our nation for military and economic help, and when we abuse that trust, we find ourselves in deep trouble. Our motives for going into Vietnam were wrong, and the way the war was conducted was wrong. If we were really sincere about helping rid the country of Communist tyranny, then why didn't we take two airplanes and bomb the dams on the Red River and Black River in North Vietnam, which would have effectively flooded out thirteen million people in less than a month and demolished their food supply. Or why didn't we go to the source of the threat and land combat troops in North Vietnam instead of the South? Our problem, from the military standpoint, was situated in the North and not the South. The questions could go on forever, but the arrogant misuse of both the military power and public trust exhibited by Presidents Johnson and Nixon was a disgrace and cost us the lives of almost sixty thousand young Americans, mostly teenagers, who didn't even know *why* they were fighting.

Finally, one must give great commendation to the young men and women who answered their country's call to arms and went to fight a very crafty, dangerous, and determined enemy on its own terms, mostly at night, and on its own soil. These young Americans gave a truly gallant account of themselves and must always be remembered for doing what they did in spite of all the hardships they had to confront and their lack of understanding of the political and military strategy involved. All three million men and women who served in Vietnam deserve their country's greatest respect.

Allen Ginsberg

Poet; antiwar activist

Vietnam was a schizo-karmic mistake. It was a mistake for this country to try to contain China, when thirty years later we would be allies.

The government was just too dopey to understand what was happening. Joe McCarthy had knocked anyone who could speak Chinese out of the State Department.

America's major early errors were seeing Russia, China, and Vietnam as a Communist monolith without historical animosities and trying to ring China with religious Christian allies who were supposed to prevent the spread of communism. The establishment of a Christian-dominated South Vietnamese government that repressed the Buddhist majority further alienated the population from its government.

American reporters in Vietnam told me that the true situation in that country was far from what the American public was being told, that contrary to what the American newspapers and media said, the Vietnamese they knew there did not really want us. They would prefer that we went away. Reporters told me that their stories were distorted at home and that the actual information was not getting through.

Arthur J. Goldberg

U.S. Ambassador to the United Nations, 1965–68

The most important lessons for students to learn from the disastrous Vietnam War are:

One, America should never be involved in a war where its vital national interests are not at stake.

Two, our country should never engage in a war that is not declared by Congress in a formal declaration, as required by our Constitution.

Barry Goldwater

U.S. Senator from Arizona, 1953–65, 1969–87

If we could have stopped communism in Asia, it would have been a gigantic step forward. Of course, we faltered on that by not stopping the Red Chinese in Korea. When Eisenhower first sent advisers to South Vietnam, with no idea of going to war, I thought it was a good thing. When President Kennedy sent fifteen thousand Marines and told them to shoot back, I was bothered, because there was no real decision made at the presidential level to win the war.

The best thing I could tell your students is that when you decide to go to war, you must at the same instant decide to win it. It's just like having a fight with another fellow: If you go into it halfheartedly, you're going to get the daylights beat out of you. That's about what happened in Vietnam. We had some brilliant victories over there, but we also had some dreadful decisions made in Washington, relative to our efforts.

Alexander M. Haig, Jr.

Battalion and Brigade Commander, 1st
Infantry Division, Vietnam, 1966–67;
Assistant to the President, Chief of White
House staff, 1973–74

First, when Alexander Solzhenitsyn was asked, following his exodus from the Soviet Union, what he would tell young Americans when he first visited the United States, he replied, "I will tell them they fought for freedom."

Second, war is serious business. God forbid that American political leaders find it necessary to consider again risking the loss of one drop of American blood in combat. But if they do, they must be prepared to decide: Is the issue, in terms of our national interest, worth the sacrifice? If so, then the decision to intervene or to apply force must be accompanied by a clearheaded determination to do all that is necessary to bring the conflict to a prompt and successful conclusion.

America's political leadership during the Vietnam War never sorted out its thinking on the first point and thereby squandered the national consensus on the second point.

Joe Haldeman

Vietnam veteran; author of *The Forever War* and *Study War No More*

Somewhere in Vietnam there may be a man about my age who nineteen years ago, with a single action, killed all of my squad but me, and put me in the hospital for five months. If I could meet him today, I hope I would be enough of a man to shake his hand and buy him a drink. He was a soldier just as we were, and that day he was a better soldier.

Somewhere in Maryland there might be a very old woman

who deep-sixed my request, as a conscientious objector, to serve my country with six years in the Peace Corps rather than two in the army. If I met her today I hope I would be man enough not to spit in her face.

Daniel C. Hallin

Author of *The Uncensored War: The Media and Vietnam*

What should kids learn about Vietnam? They should learn that we went into the war believing a lot of myths and, I hope, are wiser now. We went into Vietnam, for one thing, believing that world politics could be understood simply as a struggle between ourselves and the Communist bloc. We assumed that the Vietnamese revolution was simply a part of Moscow's global game, and that if we were tough, they would back down as the Soviets did in the Cuban missile crisis. What we didn't understand was that our opponents in Vietnam—whatever one might think of their political views—were nobody's pawn. They were fighting for their own country and weren't going to back down for anything.

We also went into Vietnam believing that war was fun and "made you a man." We grew up watching so many glorified World War II movies and playing with so many harmless toy guns that we forgot what a brutal waste of human life war is.

Morton Halperin

Deputy Assistant Secretary, U.S. Department of Defense, 1966–69; Senior Staff Member, National Security Council, 1969

The most important thing to understand about the Vietnam War is that the United States entered the war without a full debate about what our interests were. The United States should not commit forces to war without a consensus that American vital interests are at stake.

Tom Hayden

Cofounder, Students for a Democratic Society, 1961; staff, Student Non-violent Coordinating Committee, 1963; founder, Indochina Peace Campaign; member, California State Assembly, 1982–

I'm glad that your students are studying the Vietnam War. A lot of people from Oklahoma fought and died there. I don't want to preach about the losses of Vietnam. Each generation somehow discovers its own lessons. I only hope that your students demand to know the *full truth* about a conflict before they make a personal decision on whether to risk their lives. The government unfortunately did not tell us the truth about Vietnam, and they are not telling the truth about Central America today.

I wish your students a more peaceful world than that of our generation.

Larry Heinemann

Vietnam veteran; author of *Close Quarters* and *Paco's Story* (1987 National Book Award winner)

The Vietnam War was a benchmark of American history if there ever was one. It was a cusp, a strangely shaped event through which the Vietnam survivors—the whole country, for that matter—was extruded. We lost our naiveté—had it ripped out of our throats; had it beat out of us most dramatically—understanding finally that the government had betrayed us with a program of lies. Lyndon Johnson's (and for that matter Richard Nixon's) was a government of selfish, arrogant old men, jolly well ready to eat its own young, both overseas and back here, to preserve its own shabby honor and species dignity. Nixon's "peace with honor" is as hollow and shallow and laughable a phrase as Chamberlain's "peace in our time."

In its own way the Vietnam War was as extraordinary, divisive, and evocative as the Civil War—with *its* senseless blood-feud, self-destruction, draft riots, and eager but doomed young volunteers. The Vietnam War was a dirty, sloppy, ball-breaking, ugly, grueling, mean-spirited, and hateful business. And we—the soldiers in the field—learned to hate people on sight for the slant of their eyes and black pants they wore.

Parenthetically, there is nowadays circulating the oddly revised notion that the United States could have won the war. Where did this notion come from? Certainly not from any 11-Bravo grunt *I* know. To say we could have won the war is to say that we didn't fill our hearts with enough hate; didn't napalm or strafe or frag them hard enough; didn't Zippo enough hooches or turn enough of their women into whores; didn't bomb them with B-52 air strikes into small enough pieces far enough back into the stone age—the bomb craters as big as city house lots. (If we allow the same thing to happen in Central America that happened in Vietnam, it will be the shame of our lives.)

I was drafted, submitted to conscription with what can only

56

be described as soul-deadening dread, and did my tour in the Tay Ninh Province (1967–68) on an armored personnel carrier in the mechanized infantry. We rode roughshod over the countryside around Tay Ninh—Cochin China, the French called it. It seemed especially ominous and foreboding to find ruined, long-abandoned French trucks and tanks and field pieces in the jungle—abundant foliage growing out of the turrets and hatches and the horsehair seat cushions. We weren't so bone-numb exhausted and grunt-work stupid that the inference was lost on us: This is what happened to the French, and they hadn't been in Southeast Asia since 1954, what the hell are *we* doing here?

We drove ordinary convoys hell-for-leather, as the saying goes, blowing through roadside hamlets full-bore flat-out. Busting jungle—pushing over trees as big around as you can reach. Search and destroy missions—booming into back-country hamlets. For that matter, you could stand buck naked in the middle of a village street and piss in plain sight of a hundred people, and as long as you were a GI with a rifle and a steel pot, no one dared say boo. Of course it's gross. We tracked them down like dogs and shot them on sight and measured battlefield success by the particular institution of the body count, as if the corpses were so many road kills. Standing naked taking a whiz in public seems the least of our atrocities; such were the broad and generous permissions in the field. What Michael Herr said in *Dispatches* was true: we wanted to give you a Vietnam you could put in your ashtray.

The war was unwinnable in any case. Such was the Vietnamese' extraordinary ambition to rid their country of foreigners that we would have had to kill them all and burn their country to the ground. We have no reason to despise the Vietnamese for their single-minded self-determination.

In the field, if there was an overall spirit of atrocity (and it *did* take many forms), there was also another—almost opposite—spirit among the troops. I can only speak of it in this way: When Tolstoy wrote *War and Peace*, he put this perception into the mind and martial spirit of General Kutuzov, commander of the Russian armies who fought Napoleon, a fat old guy with one good eye who would fall asleep at meetings, briefings, and the like. It is the spirit of the troops, a willingness to surrender your body and your life to an idea larger than yourself (a motherland, say, or a profound and elegant democratic assumption about equality and justice), which wins a nation's war or loses it.

And if it is true that two-thirds of the U.S. troops in Vietnam were volunteers, it is also true that we soon learned of their monstrous betrayal as soon as they set foot in the field. The war was a shuck, as the saying goes, and the troops in the field understood well enough that we had been "fucked"—to say it bluntly and unmistakably.

Our most vulnerable and trusting impulses had been betrayed—squeezed out of us, burned out—by a solid year's tour, by a government that would rather kill us all than admit a mistake. We were worse than so many numbers, worse still than so many bricks in the wall, we were so much meat on the slab to be butchered. This had happened in World War I, when virtually an entire generation of men was put to death in the trenches of Europe—English, French, German, Russian; a remarkable, unconscionable waste. Indeed, the workaday, daily British casualties were tallied under the category, "Wastage."

We can metaphorically speak of the government as a "father"—who you assume loves you and wishes you only the best—and being betrayed by your own father, not once but 365 times, is a powerful, unforgettable lesson. Vietnam veterans as a rule feel used, wasted, and then dumped; many a veteran still harbors a bitterness and distrust of authority that in the years since has crusted over and hardened, but will never be ameliorated. There will always be dark places on my heart because of an almost unreasonable bitterness. It is that undeniable perception of betrayal which informs so much of the Vietnam veterans' attitudes and self-image. We are not victims and we are not heroes; there is nothing ennobling or enriching or manful about the infantry. Physically, emotionally, and spiritually we returned home reeking with what psychiatrist Robert Jay Lifton has called the "death taint," which seems a perfect word for it, and healing from the war has yet to occur.

We veterans squandered something important in ourselves. It is more than adolescent naiveté; something more than our human connection with a compassionate, regardful human world—full of cooperation, fellow-feeling, and empathy. All we can say is that we lived; we cannot say we did our work well, we cannot say that we feel good about the work we did—combat as "work" simply cannot be satisfying the way ordinary-wages work is supposed to be. War produces an astonishing, pervasive ugliness, and that's all.

On another subject. The Vietnam War divided a generation of men. I was once told by an editor of a prominent literary magazine that he felt he had missed something by not having gone to Vietnam; he assumed it was part of his manhood he missed, what used to be called a "rite of passage." He also talked about a missed literary opportunity, which I think was selfish of him, if not a little sad. I told him quite honestly that he saved himself a great deal of grief. There are those days when I would trade both my novels for these twenty years of grief. The men of my generation who opposed the war had every good reason to oppose it—their morality and the sincerity of their strong personal feeling are not in question.

I don't know that any reasonable, sensible person thinks the Vietnam War was a good and righteous undertaking, but it is crucial that we come to understand the war as an event and expression of our national character, and accept our responsibility. Now we have to discover what it was—this epoch of arrogant greed and self-destruction—and be honest with ourselves.

George Herring

Professor of History, University of Kentucky; author of *America's Longest War: The United States and Vietnam, 1950–1975*

Young people are optimistic by nature, and that is all to the good, but I think it is important for them to recognize that there are distinct limits to the power of any nation, the United States included. I think the thing that misled policymakers at each stage of the Vietnam escalation was the underlying assumption that the United States would succeed, no matter how difficult or seemingly intractable the problem was. In making decisions on such matters, therefore, we must take into account the possibility of failure and try to weigh its possible consequences. The only thing I would stress, obvious though it is, is the grimness of war. My own generation was fed a stream of John Wayne movies that painted a very romanticized, bloodless picture of war, and I fear that today's junior high school students may be similarly beguiled by such things as *Rambo.* It is important to make clear to them in the most effective way possible that war is indeed hell, and not at all the way it is often treated in the popular media, something with which you, of course, are familiar.

John Hersey

Author of *Hiroshima* and *The War Lover*

It seems to me that the lessons of Vietnam spread far beyond the borders of that country:

1. War is no way to solve problems between nations.

2. Sophisticated weapons don't win wars; the spirit and determination of the people who fight are what determine the outcome.

3. It is a mistake to think of communism as being one and the same thing in every country where it appears. Chinese communism is very different from Soviet communism; the system in each country where it appears is colored by the culture and history of that country.

4. We need to have more concern for poverty and hardship and sickness and backwardness of education in underdeveloped countries. We should be giving a helping hand rather than trying to act as world policemen.

5. So long as we preserve here at home the remarkable freedoms bequeathed to us by our Constitution and Bill of Rights, we have nothing to fear from communism. Nicaragua is not about to invade the United States. Vietnam was not a real threat to us. Cuba is not a real threat to us. We are indeed world rivals of the Soviet Union, but I believe we must contend with Russia by setting an example of democracy rather than by threatening the use of arms wherever our rival seems to be making some headway.

Seymour Hersh

Investigative journalist; author of *My Lai 4: A Report on the Massacre and Its Aftermath*

The Pentagon Papers show how Presidents Kennedy and Johnson lied to the American people and to Congress about the origins of the war.

I can think of no more important lesson—that we cannot trust our leaders to send us to kill and be killed with all the truth about our involvement.

All the lies and all the dead Americans—and Vietnamese—to support a notion of anticommunism that may not be valid. Shameful history.

Richard Holbrooke

Province Adviser and later an Executive Aide to Ambassadors Henry Cabot Lodge and Maxwell Taylor, South Vietnam, 1963–66; White House staff member, 1966–67; author of one volume of *The Pentagon Papers*, 1967; on the staff of the Paris Peace Talks, 1968–69

Vietnam was a great tragedy for our country—the most divisive event in American history since the Civil War. To be sure, our original motives were good: to help the South Vietnamese preserve their independence and freedom from Communist aggression. But our strategy was flawed and our Saigon ally corrupt and incompetent. We were fighting on unfamiliar terrain at the furthest distance from our homeland, against an enemy which, although poorly equipped, was operational in its own backyard.

It has become a cliché to say that we lost the Vietnam War at home. This is not true. The war was lost on the ground in Vietnam. Many of the dissenters and opponents of the war raised legitimate questions. The cost of the war—in lives and our national treasure, and in the effect it had on our souls—was enormous. Even if we had been able to achieve our objective, it would not have been worth it.

The Americans who fought in Vietnam were just like you and me and your students. They represented our country in both its strengths and weaknesses. They deserve our respect for their services and their sacrifice. But the leaders who planned and executed the war did not understand what they were getting into. They attempted to accomplish something that was beyond their reach in the honest belief that Americans could do anything anywhere. In this they were tragically wrong.

It is important that, in learning the lessons of Vietnam, we not lose faith in ourselves or our continuing special role in the world. We continue as a nation to stand for something special in the world, and we must not lose our optimism and confidence. The values and ideals which we stood for were correct, but it was the wrong war in the wrong place—a place we did not know.

One last point: Many of the current crop of Vietnam movies make the war seem exciting and glamorous. Well, sometimes it *was* exciting—but it was never glamorous. Tell your students that in the movies it's just acting, but in Vietnam, as you know personally, it was the real thing.

P. Evangeline Jamison

Served in the U.S. Army Nurse Corps during World War II, Korea, and Vietnam

The first and most important thing to learn about the Vietnam War is the answer to the question, Why were we there? For example, were our soldiers sent there initially as a peace-keeping force; were they sent there to stop the spread of Communism; or was there some other reason?

Second, why were our military personnel (both men and women) permitted to remain in that area for so long, making the Vietnam War our country's longest, and so costly in terms of the number of casualties?

In addition to those answers, your junior high school students should be made aware of the thousands of young lives that were lost and of the thousands who came home with physical and/or mental disabilities. It was a very costly war. The lives that were lost or were physically or mentally changed could have contributed to our country's well-being.

Another question that needs answering is, Why were the veterans of the Vietnam War, when they returned home, scorned, called baby killers, and told to go back to Vietnam and stay there?

I also feel that the roles of the ten thousand women who served in Vietnam during that conflict have not been recognized.

Darrell Johnson

Vietnam veteran, II Corps, 1968–70

My answer to your question is: Tell them the truth. Show them the photographic footage that is real. Let them see blood and guts and vomit—and tell them, "This is war—not fun! This could be *you!*"

Marvin Kalb

Correspondent; coauthor of *Roots of Involvement: The U.S. in Asia, 1784–1971* and *The Last Ambassador*

First, the political and military leaders of the United States cannot and must not lie to the American people about their major security concerns.

Second, no controversial policy can ever succeed without the support of the American people.

Third, no American must ever be called upon to sacrifice his life for a cause that is poorly understood, blurred, or deceptively explained by the administration.

Peter Kann

Reporter for the *Wall Street Journal* in Vietnam, 1967–68; now Associate Publisher, *Wall Street Journal*

I think there are several basic points students should understand.

First, how we came to be involved in the war. It happened incrementally, over many years. That's true of many events in history (and in our own lives). There is no single, big decision. Just many small decisions that lead us down a road that eventually offers fewer and fewer turnoffs and finally, in the case of Vietnam, dead-ends in a war we couldn't win.

Second, America's motives in Vietnam were entirely honorable. To help defend a society under attack. We were not there as imperialists or colonialists. We simply wanted to prevent an admittedly imperfect system and society from being changed, by force, into a totalitarian one.

Third, good intentions and efforts don't always succeed (in world affairs or in life). We had much more military might than the Viet Cong and the North Vietnamese, but we were fighting in their land and largely on their terms. And they had more patience and stamina than we had. Basically, the "good guys" don't always win.

Fourth, the war was very destructive not only in Vietnam but also in America. It divided American society, undermined faith in our political system, damaged our economy, and—a lasting effect—made it difficult, even today, to maintain public support for U.S. commitments to other small and vulnerable nations.

Fifth, if there was serious doubt about who would create a better society for the Vietnamese people—our Vietnamese allies or the Communists—there should be no doubt today. The history of Vietnam over the past decade—with its political and religious suppression, its "reeducation" camps, the tens of thousands of boat people risking their lives to flee, the poverty, and the human misery—offers convincing evidence that Vietnam would have been much better off had we been able to prevent the Communist takeover.

Ken Kesey

Novelist; author of *One Flew Over The Cuckoo's Nest* and *Sometimes a Great Notion*

The most important thing is that they know it's the same as it ever was. It hurts. Agony is agony tho' from a bullet or a broadsword. It ever hurts.

William Kimball

Vietnam veteran; author of *Vietnam: The Other Side of Glory* and *Before The Dawn*

It is imperative that we not lose sight of the human equation in war. Often we get so focused upon the contributing historical factors, the tired moralizing and political platitudes about whether U.S. involvement in Vietnam was right or wrong (an issue that will never be settled in the minds of many), that we overlook the long-term impact on the character and conscience of men and women and how they have come to terms with their participation in it and have even risen above the traumas and tragedies of their past.

My intimate involvement in the Vietnam issue and its lingering impact upon our nation has primarily been involved in offering hope and healing to those who still suffer from that painful part of our past—not through politicizing it or romanticizing it, or merely offering cathartic reflections about it, but by recognizing that war ultimately affects the deepest parts of our being and that unless we find spiritual healing and perspective, we will never truly understand this issue.

Grayson Kirk

President of Columbia University, New York, 1953–68; President Emeritus, 1968–

I would begin by pointing out that governments, like individuals, can make mistakes in judgment on policy matters. Also, once a government has made a commitment in policy terms, it is much easier, politically, to press on than to admit that a mistake has been made, e.g., the long delay before the Soviets were willing to consider withdrawal from Afghanistan.

It is important to remember that the South Vietnam problem emerged at a time when the Cold War was intense and when we assumed that communism was far more monolithic than we now perceive it to be. Our highest government officials believed that the Moscow-Peking axis was determined to obtain control over all of Southeast Asia and Indonesia, and that (the domino theory) South Vietnam was the keystone of that geographic arch.

We also believed, at the outset, that we could block the Communist drive if we gave Ngo Dinh Diem a modest amount of advisory and material aid. By 1962 we had in Saigon more than three thousand advisers and more than three hundred aircraft.

Clearly, we underestimated the skill of the experienced Viet Cong leaders, and we overestimated the prospective effectiveness of our high-technology weaponry when used under primitive conditions, a lesson one would have thought the Soviets would have learned from our experience.

The continued political weakness of the Saigon regime gradually put us in a position of greater responsibility than we had anticipated, and by 1965 President Johnson had to decide whether to abandon our whole aid policy or to introduce U.S. combat troops.

From our subsequent sad experience, I draw the conclusion that such a large-scale military operation should not have been undertaken except after a formal declaration of war, which, if obtained, would have reduced the divisive political controversy that soon developed at home and which, in the long run, was decisive in bringing about the abandonment of the whole enterprise. The American people concluded that there simply was no possible gain, in terms of the national interest, that was worth the losses we were sustaining.

Henry Kissinger

National Security Adviser under President Nixon, 1969–74; Secretary of State under Presidents Nixon (1973–74) and Ford (1974–77)

What is one to learn from our involvement in Vietnam?

1. Guerrilla wars are best avoided by preemption, by generous programs of assistance and reform in countries the United States considers vital. But once a war is in progress, victory cannot be achieved by reform alone.

2. Before America commits combat troops, it should have a clear understanding of the nature of the threat and of realistic objectives.

3. When America commits itself to military action, there is no alternative to achieving the stated objective.

4. A democracy cannot conduct a serious foreign policy if the contending factions do not exercise some restraint in their debate.

If Vietnam is to leave any useful legacy, America owes it to itself to make a fair assessment of the lessons of that tragedy. That has not yet occurred.

Radical critics seek to impose a version of history according to which bloodthirsty leaders sustained a war with no purpose except to satisfy twisted psychologies. The right distorts history by simply ignoring Vietnam. Its isolationist wing had always been more comfortable with strident anti-Communist rhetoric than with commitments to fight communism on distant battlefronts.

The lapse of more than a decade should enable America to face its past. As it turned out, the dominoes fell visibly only in Indochina. But the experience of Vietnam is deeply imprinted in the intangibles by which other nations judge America's staying power and even more in the willingness of America to defend its vital interests or even to define them. On the other hand, the Soviet Union, after a spurt of expansionism, is mired in contradictions. Vietnam, by its single-minded brutality, has turned itself into a pariah.

America failed in Vietnam, but it gave the other nations of Southeast Asia time to deal with their own insurrections. And America's very anguish testified to its moral scruples. Once again, free peoples everywhere look to America for safety and progress. Their greatest fear is not America's involvement in the world but its withdrawal from it. This is why fourteen years after the sadness of Saigon's fall, American unity is both its duty and the hope for the world.

John Stephen Knight, Jr.

High school teacher, Fairfield, Maine

Teaching about the Vietnam War to the children of those Americans who fought there, or who lived through the painful Vietnam era, is one of the most important, and difficult, jobs that an American teacher faces. The fathers and uncles of many of my students did their tour of duty there, and for many of them the war is not entirely over. Their children recognize that something important happened to their parents, but they are not sure what it is. They often sense that somehow this distant war has contributed to problems in their families, and for many it is a subject they had best not bring up at the dinner table, even though they don't know *why* they shouldn't.

I hope that students understand that no matter what the controversies surrounding our nation's involvement, the men who fought are not morally to blame for the disaster, and that we as a nation need to discuss the war and rebuild relations with Vietnam.

I want my students to develop skepticism regarding what they are told about America's foreign policy. They need to recognize that as individuals they must look behind the flag-waving and the political rhetoric and learn about the world's problems

69

from a range of sources. They should make up their own minds about what America's role in the world should be and not depend on what newspapers, television, their parents, or their teachers tell them.

There is another important lesson. Students need to see the Vietnamese not as "gooks" but as human beings who have hopes and fears and also problems left from the war. They should learn about the culture and geography of Vietnam and about its social, economic, and political problems. Students can study these topics in books, but we also need to start taking students to Vietnam—a trip which is now being sponsored by some schools.

Dennis Koehn

Served eighteen months in federal prison for resisting the draft in 1970, at the age of eighteen

First, the most important things for junior high school students to understand about the Vietnam War:

1. The war was a tragic waste of human life for both the Vietnamese and the Americans.

2. The war was carried out on a foundation of lies and deception within the U.S. military and the U.S. government. The government also lied to the American people and left a generation of Americans feeling that they will never be able to trust their government to report honestly on U.S. military and CIA activity around the world. (The U.S. media corroborated in this deception.)

3. The war was a result of U.S., Soviet, and Chinese imperialism and caused unimaginable death and suffering among the people of Southeast Asia.

4. The U.S. government abandoned our nation's highest val-

ues (democracy, liberty, equality, justice, self-determination, etc.) when it chose to support the South Vietnamese government, which had little support among the people of South Vietnam.

5. The United States contributes to a world of war, instability, and terrorism when it abandons its highest values.

6. The war was fought by middle- and upper-class policymakers sitting in offices, who sent lower-class boys to die on the battlefield. The draft during the Vietnam War was a twentieth-century manifestation of nineteenth-century slavery. Minority soldiers died in higher proportion to their presence in American society than did white soldiers.

7. Drug use among soldiers in Vietnam was very high, and in this way the war contributed substantially to drug-abuse problems in America.

8. Some soldiers went to Vietnam ready to make great personal sacrifices for what they saw as a war to promote freedom, justice, and democracy; these people should be respected and honored.

9. The United States has shamefully refused to return to Southeast Asia and reconstruct territories that it shamelessly destroyed. Our guilt weighs heavily upon our national conscience.

Second, what should we say about the men who resisted the draft and the war?

1. They were seen by most middle-aged Americans as self-centered, unpatriotic, and ungrateful cowards, but many had a great love for America and a strong commitment to its highest values.

2. Those who went to prison in a conscientious attempt to stop the war and avert a monumental tragedy are significant heroes from that period in American history. They stand proudly in the tradition of Martin Luther King, Jr.

3. Many war resisters saw the war in its reality, while the outlooks of most Americans and most political leaders were fantasies and illusions.

4. The war resisters were often middle-class intellectuals

who discovered a new side of America in federal prisons. Their understanding of America was greatly deepened and broadened.

5. Some Vietnam-era draft resisters are spiritual mentors for younger men who oppose U.S. foreign policy that abandons our country's highest values in places such as Central America, the Middle East, and South Africa.

Melvin R. Laird

Secretary of Defense, 1969–72; Domestic Adviser to the President, 1973–74

I believe the most important lesson learned from the Vietnam conflict was that the advice of President Dwight Eisenhower in 1955 should have been heeded when he stated the United States should not be involved in land warfare and land conflicts in Southeast Asia. If Presidents Kennedy and Johnson had followed this advice, there would have been no Vietnam.

Timothy Leary

Producer of psychedelic celebrations, 1965–66; wrote and acted in the film *Turn On, Tune In, Drop Out*; psychologist and author

It was a disastrous, insane, imperial invasion of a weirdo Third World country. It will leave a deep scar in the American soul for one generation.

Trust the CIA, not the military, for estimates about military events.

Marc Leepson

Vietnam veteran, 1967–68; book editor and columnist for *The Veteran* magazine

I would like to tell your students what was going on in my mind when I got drafted and was sent to Vietnam.

I got drafted into the army on July 11, 1967. I was twenty-two and had just graduated from college, but I didn't know much about what was happening in Vietnam. I knew there was a war. And I knew that the draft would catch up to me if I didn't do something to avoid it. But I felt like a leaf in the wind—as if I were at the mercy of forces over which I had no control. After a failed attempt to get into Air Force officer's training school, I sat back and let the draft catch up to me.

I went into the army willingly, knowing that I would more than likely be sent to Vietnam. I was nervous about going into a war zone, but I figured that if my country was involved, the cause must be just.

I soon learned otherwise. My feeling that I was serving my country in a good cause vanished within six weeks after I landed in Vietnam, on December 13, 1967.

By the time I'd been there six weeks I'd seen firsthand and learned from others that the massive American troop commitment seemed to be the only thing keeping the Communists from taking over South Vietnam. And the South Vietnamese Army—our ally—seemed to be riddled with corruption and incompetence, as was the South Vietnamese government.

I didn't know any GIs in Vietnam who were zealous anti-Communists. Most of us just wanted to put in our time and get home alive.

I did just that, and today I'm not certain if I did the right thing by going to Vietnam. It's not that I did anything that I'm ashamed of. But I didn't have to go, and I wound up taking part in a war that probably shouldn't have been fought.

I would ask your students to put themselves in my shoes

back in 1967, when the draft was breathing down my neck. I decided to do what I thought was my duty. But I didn't know what I was getting myself into. Perhaps if I had more knowledge of what was going on in Vietnam, I would have chosen a different path.

The country as a whole didn't know what it was getting into in Vietnam, and that's the main reason the war became a disaster. That's the most important thing for everyone to understand about Vietnam. We went into the war with little knowledge of Vietnamese history, society, or culture—or of the geopolitical situation in Southeast Asia.

We may have gone in for the best of reasons—to help a democratic country stave off communism—but we botched things terribly. Perhaps if the presidents, generals, foreign affairs experts, politicians, and American citizens in general had known more about Vietnam, Southeast Asian politics, and international communism, the United States never would have sent troops to Vietnam.

G. Gordon Liddy

Author; lecturer; businessman

The most important things for today's junior high school students to understand about the Vietnam War are:

1. Background: Indochina was a French colony when, in 1930, Ho Chi Minh founded the Indochinese Communist party. The new party was admitted into the Comintern (Soviet-sponsored international communist organization) two years later, in 1932, and set forth the goal that has guided it ever since: to establish a Stalinist state in place of French rule.

After World War II, the French tried to reimpose colonial rule. The resulting conflict resulted in a treaty, entered into at Geneva, Switzerland, in 1954, separating the ethnically different people of North Vietnam and South Vietnam into two different countries. This resulted in political entities every bit as valid as East Germany and West Germany.

In 1959, in Hanoi, North Vietnam, the Indochinese Communist party decided in its fifteenth plenum to mount a full-scale invasion of South Vietnam, and on May 19, General Vo Ban was ordered to unleash a full-scale military attack on South Vietnam to conquer it and "reunify the fatherland."

2. Type of war: The Vietnam War was *not* a "civil war." It was aggression by one state, valid politically and having ethnically different people, against another such state.

The Vietnam War was *not* a guerrilla war. It was a conventional war fought on tropical terrain. There were partisan operations on both sides as in World War II, but one will note that the victorious North Vietnamese did not enter Saigon atop mules with criss-crossed bandoliers over their shoulders. They entered as regular army divisions in Soviet tanks and armored personnel carriers.

3. The American people were consistently lied to by the press. The press, for example, reported the Tet offensive by the North as a great enemy victory. It was not. Militarily, the North was able to take but one major city (Hue) and could hold it for only three days. Politically, it was a disaster for the North. Instead of the people flocking to their banner, they fled en masse from them.

The American press helped the Communists do in the Vietnam War what the Nazi "Fifth Column" could not do in World War II—destroy the morale and fighting spirit of the American home front.

4. American military performance: Outstanding. U.S. forces rarely lost a battle, let alone a major engagement.

5. American political performance: Dismal. The politicians talked themselves into believing an oxymoron, a "limited war." There is no such thing. The Americans had no plan to win. They believed that they could discourage the enemy instead of defeat-

ing its forces and occupying its territory—the classic definition of winning a war.

6. The war was lost, ultimately, in the halls of a craven Congress.

7. Ask yourselves: If, in 1944, Betty Grable or Rita Hayworth had traveled to Nazi Germany and sat on a German 88mm flak battery (anti-aircraft gun) and cheered as it shot down an American 8th Air Force B-17 Flying Fortress bomber and had called upon General Patton's troops to throw down their arms, what do you think would have happened to her? Do you think she'd be making exercise videotapes?

Lessons:

Whenever you get involved in a war, use everything you have to fight to win—destroy the enemy and occupy its country.

In wartime the press must be controlled—as it was in World War II (by the Office of War Information).

There is no substitute for victory.

A weak and inept Congress is the best ally our enemies can have.

The responsibility for correcting all of the above falls upon your shoulders the day you become eighteen and are eligible to vote.

Don McBride

Colonel, U.S. Air Force military intelligence, retired

I could list hundreds of so-called "lessons of Vietnam." But I am now convinced that there are no real lessons of Vietnam acceptable to the entire American population. There are only historic results of the U.S. intervention in Southeast Asia. They are neither right nor wrong, moral nor immoral. They are simply what happened in Southeast Asia in a specific period.

There are basic historical facts about America's performance in Vietnam that young students should learn, but no so-called "lessons." All such "lessons" are designed in one way or another to support a certain point of view, and they have become part of the continuing controversy over what really happened.

If I were to tell a junior high school class in the simplest terms the results of U.S. activities in Southeast Asia during the 1960s and 1970s, I would say that during that period America was *vigorous* in the rapid military buildup that saved South Vietnam from internal Communist forces in the 1960s; *victorious* in all land, air, and sea battles with Communist armed forces, successfully defending South Vietnam from 1960 through 1973; and *virtuous* in the peacekeeping. Even though North Vietnam violated all its peace agreements and invaded South Vietnam with massive forces in 1972 and 1975, the United States kept its pledge to withdraw all forces. Between 1975 and 1988 it accepted almost half a million refugees from Vietnam.

I would also ask students to forget everything they think they know about the United States in Vietnam. I would tell them that most of what they may have gleaned from the U.S. media, from movies, or from war novels set in Vietnam is probably incorrect, exaggerated, or a myth. I would tell them what former President Richard Nixon wrote in the first line of his 1985 book, *No More Vietnams:* "No event in American history is more misunderstood than the Vietnam War. It was misreported then, and it is misremembered now. Rarely have so many people been so wrong about so much."

The United States fought the war against Communist aggression in Vietnam almost by chance, much like the way the great battle between General Robert E. Lee and General George G. Meade was fought at Gettysburg—because that was where the main enemy forces were concentrated. The war was fought in South Vietnam because that was where the Communist military forces were the most dangerous by the mid-1960s. That was where the Communists seemed most likely to break through the American defense perimeter in East Asia.

The primary reason the United States poured so much military, economic, and diplomatic effort into South Vietnam was to maintain the balance of power in East Asia. The tremendous American military activities in Vietnam had a much larger purpose than just aiding the South Vietnamese. Much of the U.S. effort in Vietnam was designed to have an impact on the leaders of China, Russia, Indonesia, and the other nations of East Asia and the Pacific. South Vietnam in the 1960s had become a linchpin in the U.S. efforts to maintain peace and stability in all of East Asia.

To make the situation in Vietnam easier for students to understand, I would compare South Vietnam with the original thirteen U.S. colonies. The land areas to be defended were roughly similar in size. For purposes of comparison, the exposed interior frontier of the thirteen colonies can be compared to the western borders of South Vietnam, and the coastlines of the original colonies and of Vietnam can be considered about the same length. Vietnam at many places is about one hundred miles wide. So were the settlement limits among the original colonies in the mid-eighteenth century.

This comparison gives students an idea of the area that the armed forces of South Vietnam and the United States had to defend. Then assume that the American patriots in the original colonies had to contend with large groups of Tories (or Viet Cong) who looked just like the patriots and acted like them by day but joined hostile forces to attack at night. Assume that the British (or the Russians or Chinese) could send huge amounts of arms every night to Tories along the Ohio and Mississippi rivers and the Great Lakes. Assume that these armed hostile forces attacked all settlements and towns everywhere in the colonies for years without end.

Then assume that in the midst of all this warfare, the colonists were forced to accept a new, strange form of local and national government for the first time (democracy) and had to learn to use such unusual governmental systems in the midst of the continuous warfare. This comparison will give students a good grasp of the military situation that the leaders of the United States had to face in the mid-1960s in South Vietnam.

There is another basic point for students to grasp. The American people, in their basic wisdom, have always supported the use of U.S. military force when a hostile threat becomes obvious. When people understand that a hostile threat must be dealt with militarily, the people work together to defeat or destroy it. Americans make excellent soldiers, sailors, airmen, and marines—the best in the world. Repeatedly in American history, from the pre-Revolutionary days in the thirteen American colonies to Vietnam, young Americans from farms, villages, and cities have been molded into fierce and victorious warriors by an American officer corps trained in democratic principles and beliefs.

Once a hostile military threat to some strategic area of the world is fully recognized among the American people, U.S. forces are quickly sent to block the enemy's expansion, to defeat or destroy it. U.S. forces traditionally are inserted into a blocking position against the enemy's spearheads at the last possible time. Once the victory is won or the balance of power restored, as in Korea and Vietnam, U.S. forces are withdrawn from the combat zone as soon as possible.

Once it became clear to the U.S. government by 1970 that the main Communist military threat to take over all of Southeast Asia had been blunted in South Vietnam, it was the natural desire of the American people to "bring the troops home." This feeling had been conveyed by the long-time absence of threatening acts or words by the Chinese Communists, or by the Soviets or any other Communist nations. So what happened in Southeast Asia in 1971–73 was that U.S. forces returned to their normal, permanent peacetime positions. This was to be expected, in keeping with U.S. history. The so-called antiwar movement really had little to do with the historic U.S. desire to "bring the boys home."

Another important fact that should be presented to students is that all U.S. forces—Army, Navy, Marines, and Air Force, performed magnificently in Southeast Asia. As long as U.S. forces were in Vietnam, the Communists could never win. There is no record of any U.S. military unit of any size, down to companies and platoons, that was ever defeated or that did not achieve its goal or objective.

After the 1973 peace accords, the United States completely honored its pledged word and withdrew all of its forces from Southeast Asia. The Communist government in North Vietnam almost immediately broke its pledged word. It soon became evident that North Vietnam had deceived everyone and had planned to do so when it signed the peace accords. North Vietnam constantly deceived the U.S. and various "peace" groups about its real intentions. North Vietnam quickly dishonored its solemn commitment to strive for peace. The whole world soon saw that all of what the North Vietnamese government had said, signed, and broadcast was shameless propaganda and deceit.

The whole world watched as the North Vietnamese launched another massive across-the-frontier military invasion of South Vietnam in 1974–75. They defeated the South Vietnamese armed forces, occupied all of South Vietnam, and enslaved its people. But they were able to do so only after all U.S. forces were withdrawn.

John McCain

Prisoner of War, Vietnam, 1967–73; now U.S. Senator from Arizona

Over a decade has passed since the last U.S. personnel left Vietnam. Time has given us some perspective, but the Vietnam War still presents us with some very difficult questions about the commitment of U.S. troops abroad.

Following the end of U.S. involvement in Indochina, General Maxwell Taylor stated the conditions under which he thought it was appropriate to commit U.S. troops overseas. I subscribe to General Taylor's criteria and believe these maxims must be adhered to in the wake of our misfortunes in Vietnam. First, the objectives of the commitment must be explainable to the person in the street in one or two sentences. Second, there must be clear support of the president by Congress. Third, there must be reasonable expectation of success. Finally, there must be a clear American interest at stake.

I admit that these are formidable criteria. But the stakes, the lives of young American men and women, are too great to enter into areas of conflict without substantial consideration and reason.

Paul McCloskey, Jr.

U.S. Representative from California, 1967–83; author of *Truth and Untruth*

It is possible for the United States, through the mistakes and deceit of its leaders, to be led into a bad war, in a bad place, and against the wrong people. The same is true, very possibly, with respect to the Reagan administration's policy in Central America.

Country Joe McDonald

Songwriter; singer

I guess I am most well known for singing a song at the Woodstock Music Festival in 1969 titled the "I-Feel-Like-I'm-Fixing-To-Die-Rag." I wrote the song in 1965 and never in my wildest dreams imagined that it would become one of the most famous and infamous songs to emerge from the Vietnam War era. My performance of the song at the Woodstock Music Festival was by accident. I was asked to fill time because a traffic jam was preventing performers from getting to the stage. I had actually been hired to perform with my rock band, Country Joe and the Fish, which I did on another day of the festival.

Many young people today don't know about the Woodstock Music Festival and have never heard the song. The festival was held in New York State, in the country, in the summer of 1969. It was three days long and almost all of the famous pop/rock music artists of the era performed. It attracted about 500,000 people and, due to poor planning by the promoters, became a "free" festival when the unexpectedly large audience crashed the gates the first day. It was the largest gathering of its kind in memory and was remarkable for the peacefulness of the crowd and the performers.

The words to the song, for those who don't know or may have forgotten it, are:

> Well, come on all of you big strong men,
> Uncle Sam needs your help again.
> He's got himself in a terrible jam,
> Way down yonder in Vietnam.
> So put down your books and pick up a gun.
> We're gonna have a whole lotta fun.
>
> *Refrain:*
> And it's one, two, three, what are we fightin' for?
> Don't ask me I don't give a damn,
> Next stop is Vietnam.
> And it's five, six, seven open up the pearly gates.
> There ain't no time to wonder why,
> Whoopee we're all gonna die.
>
> Come on, Wall Street and don't be slow
> Why man, this is war a-go-go.
> There's plenty good money to be made,
> Supplying the army with the tools of the trade.

Just hope and pray if they drop the bomb.
They drop it on the Viet Cong.

(*Refrain*)

Now come on Generals and let's move fast.
Your big chance has come at last.
Now you can go out and get those reds.
The only good commie is one that's dead.
And you know that peace can only be won,
When we've blown 'em all to kingdom come.

(*Refrain*)

Now come on mothers throughout the land
Pack your boys off to Vietnam,
Come on fathers don't hesitate
Send your sons off before it's too late.
Be the first ones on your block
To have your boy come home in a box.

(*Refrain*)

Since writing the song I have talked with hundreds of soldiers who fought the Vietnam War singing that song. One even told me his dying comrade's last words to him were: "Whoopee we're all gonna die." I never imagined the song would travel to the battle. I am now asked by people who have done no military service whether Vietnam veterans are angry with me for writing the song and performing it and others about the war and being an outspoken critic of the war. The truth is, I have never met a Vietnam veteran who did not like the song. One Nam vet told me that the first time she heard the song, she broke the record over her knee, but that later she got another copy and learned to love the song.

It is not a coincidence that I was able to write a song with such satirical insight. My background prepared me for it. At the age of seventeen, after graduating from high school, I enlisted in the U.S. Navy. I served three years and was honorably discharged in 1962, just before my twenty-first birthday. In addition, in my own way, I was a victim of the war between Communists and Capitalists. In 1954, when I was twelve years old, my father was investigated by the California Committee on Un-American Activities. My father, a Communist, took the fifth amendment right not to testify against himself, and in the aftermath our family suffered economic and psychological ruin. No one came to our aid during or after this ordeal (not even the American Communist party or other radical, left-wing groups). When push came to shove, we were on our own. So I wasn't just a rock star and part of the antiwar movement of the sixties and seventies. I knew what I was talking about.

People ask me if I would like to do it all over again, and many are stunned to hear me say I would *never* want to do it again. I wish there had never been a Vietnam War. A large part of my life was ruined by the war between the Communists and the Capitalists. And many, many people from my generation are dead or permanently wounded by the Vietnam War. And to this day, we, the activists, the military veterans (both men and women), the antiwar protestors, the draft dodgers, the hippies, and the yippies, are blamed for losing the war.

I would point out to young American boys and girls that, "It could be you." You could very easily be a dead Marine; a draft dodger living in Canada; a permanently disabled person in a hospital or a prison. Your life could be ruined by war. It is easy. History can just sweep you away. Events in your life can force you to think about government and war and patriotism.

An image comes to mind of a bully sitting atop a young person. Pinning down the youngster's arms and bashing him in the face, the bully yells, "Have you learned your lesson yet?" I think those who were not personally affected by the war learned almost nothing. But those of us who were affected learned one very important lesson, and that is that we don't want to get hit in the face anymore. And we don't want our children abused for national policy.

My song became an anthem of the war for good reason. My generation did not hesitate to "serve" the country. We served in the military, Peace Corps, and antiwar movement. We asked the question: "What are we fighting for?" And we never got an answer.

Because we paid, and are still paying, such a dear price, it is hard to forgive and forget. The country used and abused and then attempted to disown and discredit the Vietnam War generation. And let that be the lesson for the younger generations, so that it was not all in vain. Everyone has a right to be treated fairly and honestly. And a right to question authority. You have a right to live.

Lesson #1: Watch out for "friendly fire."

Lesson #2: It could happen to you.

Lesson #3: Peace is the only answer.

Craig MacIntosh

Infantry platoon leader, 1st Infantry
Division, Vietnam, 1968–69

I believe that Americans should *not* subscribe to the philosophy of "my country, right or wrong." We should all be interested enough to read and educate ourselves about areas of the world that our country is involved in, whether it's Asia, Central America, Africa, etc. And we should constantly question and challenge our leaders.

Robert S. McNamara

Secretary of Defense, 1961–68; President,
World Bank, 1968–81

The United States must be careful not to interpret events occurring in a different land in terms of its own history, politics, culture, and morals.

Harry McPherson

Special Assistant and Counsel to the
President, 1965–69

I'd suggest the following things about the Vietnam War:

1. The United States was drawn into it slowly, almost a decade after the French lost their former colony of Vietnam and the country was divided between North and South Vietnam.

2. In 1950–53, we had helped South Korea preserve its independence from North Korea, which was, like North Vietnam, a Communist state seeking to unify and dominate the entire country. That was a costly war, as Vietnam was, made especially so because of China's intervention on North Korea's side.

3. We sought to learn from the Korean experience not to draw China into fighting against us in Vietnam. We were also concerned that Russia might feel forced to take action against us, somewhere in the world, if we tried to conquer its junior partner and ally, North Vietnam. So we didn't try to conquer the North. We simply tried to keep the North from conquering the South. We fought a "limited" war. That made it more difficult to do the things a nation at war typically does, both on the fighting front and on the home front.

4. We overestimated the closeness of the Russians and Chinese. We underestimated the determination of the North Vietnamese. We were slow to provide our allies, the South Vietnamese, with the most modern infantry weapons they needed to fight the North Vietnamese and win.

5. In the end, the lack of a clear objective that Americans could agree upon, and were prepared to sacrifice more lives and resources to obtain, doomed the effort. That did not make the effort immoral. On the contrary, we launched it in order to defend the liberties of others—certainly a noble cause.

6. It is pretty widely believed today that the effort was unwise. Conceivably, we might have prevailed by invading a portion of North Vietnam and simply blocking the path of North Vietnam's army and weapons as they tried to move south. That

was not done out of concern that Russia would respond on behalf of its ally, North Vietnam; that world opinion would chastise us for invading a little country such as North Vietnam; and that public opinion here at home would not tolerate it.

Many brave young men died or were wounded in Vietnam. The failure of our policy did not mirror any failure of courage on their part.

There are lessons to be learned from Vietnam. It may be that one of the most important of them is that powerful nations may stumble, though their intentions are good, and that tragedy and failure are often the lot of humanity, even of the citizens of a great and favored nation such as ours.

Myra MacPherson

Author of *Long Time Passing: Vietnam and the Haunted Generation*; writer for the *Washington Post*; frequent lecturer on Vietnam and journalism

A marine called Eddie wears a wooden leg now. He looks back to that fateful day in the jungles of Vietnam. "I saw the old woman that blew my leg off. It was a command-detonated mine. I was crawlin' . . . just me and a buddy. Everyone else was dead."

For Eddie, a blue-collar kid from South Boston who went to war to "kill a Commie for Jesus Christ and John Wayne," this was not the way it was supposed to be. Like countless other teenagers, Eddie felt as invincible as John Wayne, the celluloid hero who epitomized blood-and-guts glory for the Vietnam generation. But John Wayne never got any closer to combat than Hollywood, California. Today's youth, tempted by such revisionist absurdities as *Rambo*, should know that Sylvester Stallone sat out the real war in Vietnam at a college in Switzerland.

Eddie found that war was sickeningly different from all those reels of pseudo blood. One of 350,000 GIs wounded in Vietnam, Eddie echoed a thought I have heard many times from veterans.

"I saw them World War II movies. I thought war was glorious," he said. "I thought it was glamorous."

His message to today's youth is: "Why didn't someone tell us different? Why didn't someone tell us?! War is *shit!*"

Today's youth should know what Eddie and thousands of other young men had to learn so painfully: war is not glamorous. It is only remotely tolerable and justifiable if it is deemed absolutely necessary. America's leaders, with their failed policies and reasoning, could never credibly tell us that about Vietnam.

Vietnam was an ill-conceived, ill-advised, ill-planned tragedy that left a welter of confusing legacies. With all its scars and confusions, Vietnam will haunt us forever. It is a war everyone wanted to forget—but can't. And shouldn't. By examining the unvarnished truth about Vietnam, perhaps we will learn to avoid such mistakes again.

One lesson we *must* learn is that sending young men into combat on the basis of nothing but the most abstract threats to national security is folly. Worse still is leaping into impossible situations where young men get killed for symbolic reasons. The explanation for being in Vietnam was that we were containing communism, primarily the Chinese. After all the bloodshed, destroyed land, and millions dead, the Vietnamese are fighting the Chinese, and the Chinese are our allies.

It has also never been made clear what we would have won had we beaten the North—a victory that would have necessitated keeping a large occupation force there endlessly, with the probability of the fiercely determined North Vietnamese breaking out in warfare again.

One lesson of Vietnam is that intervening is much more complicated than siding with "good guys" or "bad guys": we need to give up our delusions of omnipotence. It is not in our power to shape countries as we would want them. Rather than intervene on ideological grounds, humanitarian concerns would be better served if we asked: Will it work? Can we make life better for the country? Is it really in our national interest?

Another particularly heartbreaking lesson of Vietnam is one

that everyone would prefer to forget: it was the rankest of class wars. In this war that asked little of most and everything of a few, the blue-collar and ghetto brigades did the fighting. The best and the brightest planned that war—but they did not send their sons. This is vital to remember when one hears powerful leaders speak of Vietnam's "noble cause." If it was so noble, many now ask, why were the privileged so systematically spared? Why are no sons of congressmen or senators or presidents among those names of dead soldiers on that black granite memorial in Washington?

Particularly galling to many veterans and principled protestors is that many in the middle, who took no stand on the war but took advantage of the loopholes that kept them safe, remain smugly removed from the suffering of those who did take a stand. For the first time in our history, during the Vietnam War it became chic and righteous in influential circles not to go to war. And despite the stereotype of liberal draft dodgers, large numbers of campus conservatives who championed the war— for someone else to fight—dodged the draft and coolly charted their corporate careers.

As the young became polarized, viciousness was matched by viciousness. Nurses who went to Vietnam only to help were shunned when they returned home. Veterans were seared by hostile homecomings. Veteran Fred Downs was walking across campus when a student noticed the hook that had replaced his hand. "Get that in Vietnam?" When Downs nodded yes, the student sneered, "serves you right." On the other side, hard hats beat up war protestors. And a marine recalls that after the National Guard killed four students during an antiwar protest at Kent State, a cheer erupted when someone scrawled on the blackboard in a class at Quantico, Kent State 0, National Guard 4. Even parents were treated with unbelievable callousness. The mother of a dead soldier received an anonymous telephone call after her son's funeral. "You got what you deserve. He had no business being there."

While there are odious tales of hypocrisy and cruelty from that era, it is wrong to blame an entire generation of men for their choices. The blame rightly belongs with the misbegotten war and the politicians. One of the most shameful aspects of our Vietnam policy was Project 100,000—the deliberate drafting of those with marginal lives and minds. Ostensibly, the purpose of this Great Society program, which lowered mental and physical recruitment standards, was to provide training and discipline to America's disadvantaged youths. The program, however, became a vehicle for channeling poor youths to Vietnam's front lines. The promised programs to teach new skills seldom materialized for these recruits, often tagged the Moron Corps by fellow soldiers. (The Army, for example, took some with IQs as low as 62.) And it is rarely mentioned that a disproportionate number of Project 100,000 men died in combat, and that they were disproportionately black. Nor is it mentioned that Project 100,000 helped stave off the politically nettlesome prospect of dropping student deferments or calling up the National Guard or the reserves.

That these past inequities are not yet buried was demonstrated by the furor Vice-President Dan Quayle's National Guard service created during the 1988 presidential campaign. Quayle championed the Vietnam War but chose a path that all but assured he would not have to fight. Vietnam combat veterans, stung by Quayle's record in Congress of voting against increased benefits for veterans, watched helplessly as the Republican campaign turned the country's wrath against the media, charging that it had impugned the patriotism of all national guardsmen by questioning Quayle. The tactic successfully obscured for many Americans the well-documented fact that the guard was a class sanctuary during Vietnam. For many veterans it was just another bitter pill: the message is that privilege paid off then and still does today.

The class aspects of the Vietnam War are central to understanding the duplicity of national policy then and why so much rancor remains, but in a more personal way, many on both sides of that war have similar legacies—alienation and cynicism about American politics and ambiguity about their youthful decisions or about the war. The generation that believed in John F. Kennedy's "ask not what your country can do for you" call to patriotism experienced a profound sense of betrayal.

All told, the Vietnam War defies common experience. Yet there were general aspects of combat that must be explained to today's youth. In this war of no fixed goals, the "body count" became a perverted measurement for winning. Units were awarded ice cream and beer for killing the most. Years later, men faced the trauma of being part of such purposeless killing. In a war with no front lines, fought in and around civilians, it was often impossible not to kill them. Years later, soldiers remember the bloodied bodies of women and children. They never knew who the enemy was. Friends were ripped apart by an invisible enemy—the booby trap. GIs went in one-year hitches. Survival guilt developed years later when they wondered what happened to those who remained behind.

They were teenage warriors, statistically six years younger than those in World War II. Instead of a carefree adolescence, their first sexual encounters often were with prostitutes in Vietnam. Many had trouble relating to women when they returned. Youth often has fewer coping skills: death of friends hit them harder than if they had been older. There was no such thing as troop-ship decompression; in America's first jet-age war they were back "in the world" in hours. One helicopter pilot told me, "I was killing gooks in the delta and seventy-two hours later I am home in bed with my wife—and she wondered why I was different."

Such guerilla warfare is what today's youth would experience, because atomic weapons have made all-out victories such as World War II obsolete. Instead, the superpowers will have to continue to fight their "dirty little wars," as Vietnam was termed, and as Afghanistan became for the Russians; surrogate wars of bluff and bloodshed in tiny countries around the world.

If such wars recur, America would face a major cost never written in the defense budget—the cost of creating new veterans. For a trenchant lesson of what happens to soldiers of unpopular wars, we can look to the shameful treatment of Vietnam veterans. Congress refused to appropriate adjustment counseling funds for a decade, Vietnam veterans were treated to one of the shabbiest GI bills in history, and Reagan's administration tried to gut their counseling centers and stalled a congressional order to study the effects of Agent Orange.

The private sector was little better. For years, frustrated veterans urged businessmen in vain to hire Vietnam vets. And America's Vietnam Memorial was not the gift of a grateful nation. Veterans themselves had to raise the money.

A final lesson would be for every junior and high school class to visit the Vietnam Memorial. There, tourists still their talk and laughter. Veterans in wheelchairs stroke the indentation of names, almost as the blind finger Braille. Roses, pictures, letters are placed beside names: "This is my father. I never knew him. If anyone knows him, please write me."

It is important for the young to look at those names, wall upon wall, nearly 58,000 of them, and realize that this is the highest of all the prices of that war. Reconciliation and understanding can come only if the vast majority, those of us relatively untouched by that war, take it upon ourselves to face what it all meant. This means, in part, listening—and listening *hard*—to the tales that those of the Vietnam generation have to tell.

Ben Maddalena

Interested citizen; student of national and international problems for forty-five years

My suggestions for educating today's students about Vietnam are:

1. The United States should have never escalated its involvement in Vietnam further than the adviser stage.

2. Any full-scale involvement should have been in Thailand, where the people were united and willing to defend their country.

3. No serviceman in the Vietnam War or in any other war died in vain if he served in good faith.

4. The president, the Congress, and the people all failed and all share the blame for the involvement.

5. People should examine history to learn what to do.

6. The war brings up a matter that has a broader scope, mainly, what should be done to solve our national problems. Since the Truman era, the United States has not been using rational judgment in solving national or international problems. People need to realize that only by better understanding and better efforts from themselves can matters such as the elimination of war or the attainment of social and economic progress be effectively dealt with by the government. No president can accomplish this alone, as it is not humanly possible.

A single mind has the capacity of a present-day computer fifty stories high and covering an area the size of the state of Texas. We have 200 million minds out there ready to solve problems if asked. The president should be able to present the entire nation with specific problems, such as how to solve the national deficit, how to solve the foreign trade deficit, how to improve social values, what our national goals are, and how to achieve the best peace.

Since the end of World War II, failure to successfully meet the national and international problems of the nation is due not to a failure of the president or Congress but to failure of the people of our nation. History will repeat itself forever unless people become better informed and unless they provide the necessary support and input to the president and Congress. It is the people, not the administrations, that have been flawed. The Vietnam War is merely a part of the evidence of this fact.

Thomas H. Moorer

Chief of Naval Operations, 1967–70;
Chairman, Joint Chiefs of Staff, 1970–74

The Vietnam War was a political war that imposed restraints upon the military that prevented the use of power that was readily available. This meant that the war dragged on and on, to the point that it was no longer supported by the public and was underfunded or not funded by the Congress.

President Johnson made three points: (1) We will not overthrow Ho Chi Minh; (2) we will not invade North Vietnam; and (3) we seek no wider war. With respect to number one, the only reason for entering a war is to overthrow a government that is doing something we cannot accept. Consequently, the primary objective should have been to overthrow Ho Chi Minh.

With respect to number two, I believe Vietnam is the only country that involved itself in a war and was able to employ all divisions since it finally concluded that we would never invade North Vietnam. Furthermore, it forced our ground troops to fight in South Vietnam, where it was difficult to tell friend from foe, hence, the Calley affair.

With respect to number three, the politicians were so afraid that China and Russia would enter the war that they imposed limitations and restraints on our military people that placed them in jeopardy. For instance, the fear that we might damage or even kill a citizen of China or Russia never allowed them to bomb the airfield at Hanoi—so the North Vietnamese had a sanctuary on which to base their best fighter aircraft.

Tell your junior high school students that when they grow up, they must never permit politicians to enter a war they do not intend to win.

John D. Negroponte

Second Secretary for the Department of
State in Saigon, 1964–68; U.S. Delegate to
the Paris Peace Talks, 1968–69; National
Security Council staff, 1970–73

I think the most important thing for your students to know about the Vietnam War is that, although our involvement was indeed for a worthy cause, the United States lost. As painful and difficult as this may have been for our country to accept at the time, it was unlikely that our country could have maintained an undefeated record indefinitely. In that sense, our loss was an inevitable part of a national maturation process.

Another point is that of all the tactical mistakes we made perhaps the most serious was to take on too much of the fighting of the North Vietnamese main force units ourselves, leaving the South Vietnamese to defend the villages. In other words, we started the Vietnamization process far too late. But most important of all, I think we picked a difficult fight in a very far away place. I am sure the results will help ensure that we pick our fights more carefully in the future.

Donald Oberdorfer, Jr.

National correspondent, *Washington Post,*
1968–72; Northeast Asia correspondent
based in Tokyo, 1972–75; author of *Tet*

The United States, which emerged from World War II by far the strongest power in the world, was under the misimpression until Vietnam that its power was unlimited— that it could accomplish anything anywhere in the world if it seriously undertook to do so. Vietnam proved this not to be the case. Whether because the task was impossible from the start or because it was poorly executed or because in the end the American people lost confidence and terminated support—and I think there were elements of all three—the Vietnam War was a monumental failure of a giant-scale national project. America has (thank goodness) had few such failures in modern times. (The Depression was another, in a different area.) Therefore it has left powerful emotions and angry scars.

Lawrence F. O'Brien

Special Assistant to Presidents Kennedy and Johnson

The cause was just, America's stake was high, and the outcome represented a serious setback for our nation. The tragic loss of lives and the divisions and bitterness should teach us that regardless of the justification of the cause, we cannot engage in war without the overwhelming support of our people and a total commitment to succeed.

Tim O'Brien

Author of *Going After Cacciato* and *If I Die In A Combat Zone*

I'd say it's most important to teach young students about the moral ambiguities of the war in Vietnam; how difficult it was to separate right from wrong on any given issue. For each argument in favor of the war, there seemed to be an equally compelling counter-argument, and in the end most Americans were left with an abiding sense of uncertainty and moral confusion. Men were

96

being killed, and were killing, but there was no sense of a national moral consensus—"certain blood for uncertain reasons"—a quote from one of my books. And I think it might be wise to ask students whether a nation ought to go to war with such a sense of ambiguity about what's right and wrong.

Charlton Ogburn, Jr.

Author of *The U.S. Army* and *The Marauders*

Many people have said that the commitments of our government required us to come to the defense of the Saigon regime. Whatever our commitments to that regime may have been, we had a previous and far more weighty commitment, made before the world, not to do what we did in Vietnam, which was to intervene unilaterally in another country with military force to make our will prevail there. Our invasion of Vietnam lacked any sanction by the international community or by any body conceivably to be regarded as representative of the Vietnamese people. The Americans who died in two world wars and the Korean war died essentially for the principle that the nations of the world should be secure from just such intervention—from aggression. The government sacrificed the lives of more than fifty thousand young Americans to vitiate the principles for which those 400,000 were sacrificed.

A century from now we shall still not have lived down the needlessness, the duplicity, the barbarity of our adventure in Vietnam.

George S. Patton

Military Assistance Command, Vietnam,
1962–63; Commanding Officer, 11th
Armored Cavalry Regiment, Vietnam,
1968–69; Major General, U.S. Army, retired

Briefly, the most important points are the following:

1. There was an absence, almost total, of a national strategy, which should have been promulgated by the White House in conjunction with the secretary of defense and the joint chiefs of staff. What was announced suffered many changes as the war went on. There were reasons for this, one being a fear of intervention by the Chinese Communists.

2. All nine principles of war were violated from time to time. These are listed below, and those that were vital to the pursuit of that war are underlined:

Objective
Economy of Force
Mass
Surprise
Unity of Command
Security
Offensive
Maneuver
Simplicity

I would add to those nine principles that of cultural understanding. It was also violated, because in most cases, it simply did not exist.

3. Lyndon Johnson failed to mobilize either the Armed Forces or the people at home. In other words, business as usual was the byline. There was no rationing and no reserve or National Guard call-up until after February, 1968. Even then, it was minimal.

4. In 1962–65, the Military Assistance Command, Vietnam (MACV) and the American Embassy lied to the press and hence alienated them. They failed to realize the mobility of the press in that war, through the use of helicopters.

5. The most important point your students must obtain is that because of our defeat in so-called limited warfare by an

eighth-rate power (if that high), our enemies have discovered an Achilles heel and are putting it to us in Central America today. We have demonstrated a weakness in this type of conflict, and they are capitalizing on that weakness. Because of that, some blood may be spilled in that area in the future, *if we have to invade.* Cuba is the problem—*not* Nicaragua.

Tom Paxton

Songwriter; singer; antiwar spokesman

I would attempt to teach junior high school students that the Vietnam War was the first American war fought without broad popular support, that, indeed, opposition was so widespread that some dissenters were so misguided as to belabor veterans like yourself—a definite first in U.S. wars. It was an unwinnable war because the Viet Cong had broad popular support and there was pervasive corruption on the part of the South Vietnamese government. One can detest communism (as I do) and still say that since the overwhelming majority of the Viets either wanted it or didn't care, there was no hope of forestalling it.

I'm glad you made it home.

Jeff Perez

Helicopter doorgunner, Vietnam, 1967–68

Most of the people who went to Vietnam behaved in a professional manner. A lot of people have the wrong impression of the Vietnam veteran. He's not a psycho who could go crazy at any time, and he's no Rambo. The men who went to Vietnam were just ordinary guys—even the ones who won tons of medals.

When I went into the service at age seventeen after completing high school, I wanted to go to Vietnam. I was raised to believe that you pay a price to live in this country, and the price is that whenever there is a war or a conflict, or whatever you want to call it, you go. It's your duty. Some people call it corny or even stupid. I call it the right thing to do. People may laugh at my opinion, but that's the way I feel. When I get up in the morning and look at myself in the mirror, I can say to myself, "Jeff, you did the right thing. You've got nothing to be ashamed of. You should be proud of yourself for what you did." And I am.

As for the protestors, I respect the ones who really believed in what they were protesting and were willing to leave their families. A lot of people talk bad about the boys who went to Canada. But I don't hate them. If they really believed in what they were doing, then more power to them.

Ed Perkins

Professor of History, University of Southern California

When I was in junior high school, I believed that every American president always told the truth in speaking to the American public on radio or TV. But during the Vietnam War, when I was in my late twenties and early thirties, I heard two presidents, Johnson and Nixon, one a liberal and the other a conservative, repeatedly lie to me and the entire American public about events in Vietnam, just like Hitler lied to the German people during the World War II era. On the basis of those lies, thousands of Americans only a little older than a junior high school student were sent to be killed or maimed in Vietnam, and all for no valid reason, win or lose. As you get older and pay more attention to national and international events, you should cultivate a skeptical attitude about the speeches and pronouncements of presidents, no matter what their political philosophy, and especially when they are discussing the alleged reasons for military action overseas. Political leaders are more likely to distort the truth about places far away because it is more difficult for you and other citizens to discover the real facts. Skepticism is not unpatriotic, because so often in the past overseas military attacks on Americans have proved to be exaggerated, manufactured out of thin air, or even deliberately provoked by prior U.S. military action.

John Clark Pratt

Author of *Vietnam Voices: Perspectives on the War Years, 1941–1982* and *The Laotian Fragments*

_____

The war didn't just "happen"—as did American participation in World War I, World War II, and Korea. We became involved gradually, starting in 1953 and escalating in 1960–64—but all the time secretly, as two administrations kept the public in the dark about what was really going on, and the Oliver Norths of those days were allowed to do their own things. By the time the American people found out about the war, we were already so deeply involved that there was no turning back.

The other side of this problem, however, is that the American public *could* have known, if people had cared enough to read and think. But they didn't, preferring not to believe that by 1963, for instance, we had sixteen thousand troops in Vietnam, even though we said we didn't.

Moral: Don't depend on televised hearings to let you know what's going on. Read everything. Find out for yourself. Don't believe the visual media. *Work* at being a member of a free society. If you don't, someone else may well cause you to lose your freedom.

Okay? The parallels to Central America should be obvious. I'm definitely against covert wars, believing as I do that if it's good enough to fight for, it's worth telling the truth about.

Nicholas Proffitt

Newsweek Bureau Chief, Saigon, 1972; author of *Gardens of Stone*

The most important things for today's young people to understand about the Vietnam War are:

1. The Vietnam War was a failure. Not just because the United States did not come away with a victory, but because all wars are failures. When a nation goes to war, it means that leaders on both sides failed to resolve their differences by peaceful and civilized means.

2. War is not glamorous. Junior high school students are of an age when young boys (girls seem to have much more sense) are inclined to see glory in war. They play war. They watch war movies on television. They spend hours drawing pictures of tanks and airplanes and bloody battles. Try this instead: First draw a picture of your father lying dead on the ground; then draw a picture of your mother burying your baby brother or sister. Does war still look glamorous?

3. There were no "good guys" or "bad guys" in Vietnam. There were good people and evil people on both sides of the battle line. You know the story of the American Revolution. To most of the Viet Cong and North Vietnamese soldiers, we Americans were the British. They were the Americans.

4. There was, and is, no Rambo.

Thomas R. Pullen

Helicopter pilot, Hue, Vietnam, 1967–68

Learn all you can about the war in Vietnam. Research the reasons for U.S. involvement. Study the personalities and political motivations of the people who made the decisions that resulted in our involvement. Then use the power of your vote to assure that it will never happen again.

Mr. and Mrs. Ed Pulliam

Parents of Eddie Pulliam, killed in Vietnam, 1970

All we can say is . . . tell the truth. The Vietnam War was a political war. Our boys had no business being over there. However, we taught our son to be patriotic and to honor his God and his country. We live in a wonderful country, and nowhere else in the world do people have the freedoms we enjoy today.

At the time our son went into the service, he did not know the facts about the war. Neither did we. He went to fight for our freedom. A lot of questions are still unanswered today.

Our son wrote a letter home before he was killed, in which he stated that he would be dead by the time we received the letter. He knew that he was going on his last mission, but he said that he was dying for his country and his family. He believed in what he was doing and his dying was not in vain.

The Vietnam War was a terrible waste, but so is any war.

Allen Repp

Vietnam veteran, 1966–67

I don't consider myself a superpatriot, but I did go to Vietnam because I *wanted* to go. I saw enough to leave me with a lifetime of questions. When I came back from Vietnam, I was completely confused about what was going on here in the United States. I started researching the war immediately and have continued to do so ever since. I served proudly and would do it again, but I *need* to know *why*.

I offer the following lessons learned in Vietnam.

1. Though our invasion and supply lines to Vietnam stretched halfway around the world, we had the best-fed and best-supplied troops in the history of warfare.

2. Mass warfare can be waged, and mind boggling numbers of enemy killed, without nuclear weapons or the threat of world war.

3. Russia and China are not nearly as eager to confront the power of the United States as we had been led to believe.

4. A majority of the public can be totally misinformed and led in whatever direction may be the whim of the news media.

5. The United States is, and always will be, the number one military power in the world. Freedom/Patriotism is the key.

Elliot L. Richardson

Secretary of Defense, 1973; U.S. Attorney General, 1973

There are at least two important things that today's junior high school students should understand about the Vietnam War. First, they should understand that the United States should never undertake a military action that cannot, whether for military or political reasons, be successfully carried out. Second, because there are many situations like Vietnam and Nicaragua where decisive U.S. military action is not appropriate or feasible, the United States needs to exert effective leadership in pursuing alternative means of protecting its security interests through cooperative multilateral means.

William P. Rogers

U.S. Secretary of State, 1969–73

Whatever the verdict of history may be about the participation of the United States in the Vietnam War, all Americans can be proud that our motive was in no way selfish, but was intended to give the people of Vietnam the right to determine their own future.

Lionel Rosenblatt

Adviser in the U.S. pacification program in South Vietnam, 1967–70; now a legislative management officer, U.S. State Department

To me there are two key lessons of the Vietnam War:

1. The United States should not get involved if the government we are backing has fallen below a certain level of competence, honesty, and popular support. In the case of Vietnam, our involvement also faced an added difficulty—the appearance (however unjustified) that we were following in the French footsteps as colonizers, with the government of South Vietnam as our puppet.

2. The above difficulties notwithstanding, I believe that we had a chance to win the war. Certainly, a majority in South Viet-

nam did not want the Communists to take over. We failed, however, to stimulate in the government of South Vietnam the political and administrative reforms necessary to command strong popular support. To put it another way, after removing Ngo Dinh Diem, we were gun-shy about trying to change the Vietnamese political scene, even though leadership at the top was lacking. For some reason, we were far more ready to intervene with military power than with political leverage; in reality the two must go in tandem.

From 1967–70, on the ground in Vietnam, I always grew gloomy about our prospects in the war when South Vietnamese counterparts would ask why the United States was unable to influence a better quality in the top military and civil officials in Saigon and the countryside. Ironically, our involvement actually fed corruption, because of all the largesse we brought into the war effort; appointments of South Vietnamese government officials were made not on merit but for a fee.

Some say that we should have fought harder militarily. I believe that the way to victory was through forging a tougher, more effective partner in the government of South Vietnam, which meant being willing to fight as hard for improved political and administrative performance as we did on the military front. Unless our future allies can compete with the Communists for popular support, no amount of military muscle can salvage the situation.

The more than one million Indochinese refugees who have fled the Communist regimes there in the past fourteen years are ample proof that we had the potential support of most Indochinese for a free Laos, Cambodia, and Vietnam. The governments we supported were not up to the job, and we gave insufficient emphasis to effecting an improvement in their performance.

Dean Rusk

Secretary of State, 1961–69; Professor, University of Georgia School of Law

The most important question connected with the Vietnam War is how we are to organize a durable peace in a nuclear world. We cannot achieve peace just by hoping for it but must make an organized effort to take appropriate action when the armed battalions begin to move. Collective security is more than a slogan; it is the pillar of peace in the world today.

We can take real satisfaction that it has been over forty years since a nuclear weapon was fired in anger, despite the many crises we have had since 1945. I reject the Doomsday talk with which we are battering young people these days. We are accustomed to being very critical of political leaders in both the United States and the Soviet Union. Nevertheless, we should bear in mind that these leaders are not idiots when it comes to nuclear war. The record is to the contrary.

Pierre Salinger

Press Secretary to Presidents Kennedy and Johnson, 1961–64; now chief foreign correspondent, ABC News

Students should understand that our participation in Vietnam drastically changed the attitude of Americans about participating in overseas wars.

It was the first war in the history of the United States in which the veterans who returned home were not treated as heroes, and it was the first war in the history of the United States that did not have vast public support. The consequence of that war has alerted the American public to press for the nonparticipation of the United States in overseas conflicts.

Harrison Salisbury

Assistant Managing Editor, *New York Times*, 1964–72; Associate Editor, 1972–74; author of *Behind The Lines: Hanoi*

I think the way to get kids interested in the Vietnam War is by personal tales. You are a veteran, and when you tell students of your experience, it means something. You are a live person who fought there. There has to be reality to it. I am afraid that to junior high school students the war has drifted off into the clouds, as the Korean one did before, and World War II. All that is left are some remnants of cheap comedy on television and some fake melodrama.

I can't think of any slick answer. It was a tough war for everybody, and when you look back at it your wonder mounts—that it was fought, that the country divided, that it stopped, and that we still don't really know why we did it.

Sorry not to have something short and smart, but that wasn't the kind of thing it was, and don't you ever believe we aren't still paying for it, and the kids will too.

Neta Sanders

Mother of Phillip Sanders, killed in Vietnam, 1970

It's very hard for me to express my feelings about Vietnam to myself or to my family. The propaganda (especially of the last few years) has left me feeling quite empty. I never knew losing someone you loved could hurt so badly for so long; however, comments such as, "The soldiers in Vietnam died for no reason" tend to throw salt on my wounds. Whether the war was right or wrong—based on our nation's security or a leader's pride—the men who fought, were wounded, and died were very much in the right and should be showered with nothing less than the glory and honor they deserve. We as a nation must stop grieving and glorify those who (in at least their and their families minds) fought to protect the freedoms we so often take for granted. Our children must be taught at an early age to respect those who cared enough to fight. So far the people who have taught our youth about the war have been Hollywood producers. This is not entirely bad, because it did bring the Vietnam conflict into our young people's lives. Now it is up to us to educate our youth on each and every part of the war. We should hide nothing— even if it means making our government look dumb.

In my very own opinion I feel the Vietnam war should never have been fought, but I also realize that my opinion is clouded by my son's death. The things that our youth are taught must be unbiased by either opinion of the war. In short, we should give them the truth and hope and pray that they are intelligent enough to understand and put the things they learn to use. No one should have to lose a loved one and then be abused by such controversy. Our young people are our future, and only they are responsible for the future; however, we should not send them into the future blind. They deserve the truth, good or bad.

Arthur Schlesinger, Jr.

Author and historian; Special Assistant to the President, 1961–64

Today's junior high school students should understand that it is a great mistake for the United States to get involved in any war beyond its zone of direct and vital interests. We are not world saviors—either in Vietnam in the 1960s or in the Persian Gulf in the 1980s.

R. L. Schreadley

Special Assistant to the Commander of
Naval Forces, Vietnam, 1969–70

American military forces should never be committed to an extended campaign without the clear intent to achieve victory and without the express support of Congress and the American people.

Pete Seeger

Folksinger; composer; antiwar spokesman

I think I would tell any young person that the Vietnam War, like many wars, was basically undertaken for economic reasons. President Eisenhower himself said, "The United States must have access to tungsten, which can only be got from China and Vietnam." There are many dictatorial governments in the world, many much worse than the government of Vietnam. But we don't see the U.S. government planning to invade them and set up a puppet government. Of course, we do interfere often in various covert ways.

The second important thing to remember about Vietnam is that modern science has put the entire human race on the brink of disaster. Not only the whole human race but perhaps all life on earth could be wiped out if the wrong buttons get pressed. I don't think anybody in our country should shrug his or her shoulders and say, "Well, there's nothing I can do about it." We can vote; we can write letters; we can learn; we can argue. We are fortunate in this country to have some very wonderful laws, among them the Bill of Rights to the U.S. Constitution.

Paul Shannon

Editor, *Indochina Newsletter*

First, it is critical for students to know that the Vietnamese are not our enemy—they never were and they are not today. For well over forty years the Vietnamese have wanted to be our ally, fighting with us in World War II and turning to us for help thereafter. It is important to get to know these people as they are, not as the media and movies today present them. We have much to gain from offering the hand of friendship to these people at last. Only when we do will the war be over for us. And, since the Vietnamese have been unable to pull themselves out of poverty, they could really use our help rather than our hatred.

Second, we have to know why these people were turned into our enemy. We have to put aside all this nonsense about communism versus democracy and find out what it was about these people that made very powerful interests in this country fear them so much and try to stamp out their social movement. When we understand why we were tricked into fighting these people we will cry and be angry and understand many things. We can then redefine for ourselves who are our friends and who are our enemies, based on our own values and on what we want our lives to be like. If we reject our friends, thinking they are our enemies, we will pay a very high price.

Third, it's worth investing your time in studying this war in great detail instead of accepting what people say about it. You will be surprised by what you find. There are certain events in history that, when studied, teach us incredible things about our world, our country, and ourselves that we just won't learn otherwise. The Vietnam War is one of those events. Look into it. Listen to what everyone has to say, but focus on the history as well. Then make up your own mind.

Evelyn Sloat

Mother of Donald Sloat, killed in Vietnam, 1970

I have started at least eight different answers to your question. To even think about this war grieves me very much.

It grieves me to think about the young men of America who were willing to serve because of their loyalty to this country. These young men gave their lives or suffered hardships and anguish during this long war against the Communists, and then were brought home by the politicians, only to be shunned and ignored by their nation. This made many of them think they were a disgrace to America.

As citizens of the United States we have a duty to ourselves to be learned, informed, and active about what our government leaders are doing in Washington.

If we are to fight a war, we should support our fighting men and put forth a 100 percent effort to win. Then we should recognize those who deserve to have their praises shouted for having given their all in service to their country.

Lillian M. Snyder

Professor emeritus, Western Illinois University, Macomb, Illinois

My brother, a second lieutenant who had just graduated from the University of Illinois, was assigned during World War II to the U.S. Army Signal Corps in the South Pacific. In the course of its duties my brother's unit received much help from the people of Vietnam while it was assigned in that area. Ho Chi Minh was a staunch supporter of the United States throughout the war. He was an admirer of American democracy.

112

At the end of the war my brother's unit visited Hanoi. The citizens had decorated all the lamp posts with roses and welcomed the troops as they marched through the city. Ho Chi Minh explained to my brother how much his country had suffered and how they would need help in building their democracy. He wondered if the United States would help them in this effort. My brother, as head of his company, could see their need and hoped the help would be forthcoming. Ho Chi Minh gave my brother his picture. There was much elation in the celebration of the victory of the Allied Forces of World War II.

But help was not forthcoming. Vietnam was not free to rebuild its country. What went wrong? This question is still unanswered in my mind. Perhaps your students can find the answer. Ho Chi Minh was forced to borrow money from whoever would lend it.

According to the press, Ho Chi Minh accepted a loan from Russia, the only country willing to assist Vietnam in developing its agriculture.

When my brother read about this in later years, he tore up Ho Chi Minh's picture.

Why didn't we help Vietnam in 1945 when the people needed it?

Theodore Sorensen

Special Counsel to the President, 1961–64

As support from the U.S. public declined, limited U.S. military intervention could not successfully maintain in power a South Vietnamese government whose undemocratic methods lost the support of its own population; and unlimited (i.e., nuclear) intervention would have achieved nothing, while destroying all Vietnam, America's honor and reputation, and possibly the world.

Shelby L. Stanton

Vietnam veteran; military historian; Senior
Editor, *Vietnam* magazine; author of
Vietnam Order of Battle

The Vietnam War was a bitter and complicated experience for the entire nation as well as for those who fought there. It is important to always remember, however, that with few exceptions the Americans and their South Vietnamese comrades who served at the front did so with great bravery—despite the great personal dangers involved and the unpopularity of the war. The country can always be proud of the tremendous courage and fighting valor of its citizen-soldiers in that long and difficult war. The country should also be grateful for the Vietnamese who came here after the war, because many of their parents fought very bravely to defend their freedom.

After Vietnam, the South Vietnamese soldiers were called cowards, and the U.S. soldiers were thought of almost as criminals. For the most part, this was unfair. The motivations of our national leaders are sometimes complicated. During the Vietnam War, both South Vietnam and the United States drafted young men to fight because it was the law, and most responded obediently. They did not ask why or give excuses, but did their jobs as best they could. They trusted the leaders of both nations to be right. Many were teenagers when they were killed or maimed. Some Vietnamese soldiers were even younger.

War is a terrible thing, and elected officials must decide carefully whether anything is worth such a terrible cost. But there are times in which service to the country is worth the price exacted. Our Revolution and Civil War are good examples. Vietnam is less clear, but no matter how history will judge the war's results, let there be no doubt that the soldiers, sailors, marines, and airmen in Vietnam performed their jobs with exemplary valor and pride. Sometimes it is not popular to do the right thing, and people will laugh and question you for doing it. To place the greater welfare of the country above your own is the greatest sacrifice a community can demand. Those who answered their country's call, both in Vietnam and in the United States, were patriots and heroes of the highest caliber.

Jerold Starr
Director, Center for Social Studies Education

Unlike in the movies, few soldiers are challenged to be heroes in war. Most of the time they are bored, because there is nothing to do, or very frightened, because their lives are in jeopardy and there is little that they can do to protect themselves.

All wars destroy, and Vietnam took a heavy toll in lives, treasure, and spirit. Over 58,000 young Americans were killed, 300,000 were wounded, and almost 14,000 completely disabled. Haunted by the war's horrors and rejected by an ungrateful public, some 700,000 veterans have had "significant" to "severe" problems of readjustment.

In Vietnam today over two million dead are mourned. The once green landscape is pockmarked with 26 million bomb craters. Almost 5 million acres of forest and croplands were laid waste by 18 million gallons of poisonous chemical herbicides.

This terrible toll of death and destruction cost American taxpayers hundreds of billions of dollars, and we will continue to pay billions more in costs such as veterans benefits and interest on past loans. In short, the wounds of war last for decades, even generations, beyond the last battle.

Nations do not go to war because human beings are naturally violent. On the contrary, the most difficult task of any nation at war is to recruit and train soldiers who will risk their lives in combat. Rather, a nation goes to war because its political leaders decide that, despite the predictable casualties, it is in the nation's interest to do so. A nation might go to war for the following objectives: to increase its *power* or to prevent its enemy

115

from increasing its power; to defend or advance its *prestige*, that is, its standing in the eyes of the world; to enforce cherished *principles*, such as ensuring human rights or the rights of vessels at sea; for *profits*, that is to advance its economic interests by protecting investments, securing raw materials, or gaining new markets for its exports; or to *protect* its people and territory from attack.

At different times, different U.S. officials cited all of the above objectives to explain U.S. policy in Vietnam. However, very few people were ever convinced that U.S. power, prestige, principles, profits, or protection were ever at stake in the conflict that divided the small, distant, and less developed country of Vietnam.

Moreover, it is important to note that, often, going to war is not the most effective way for a nation to achieve its goals. Other policies might offer as much chance of success with far less risk. For example, some in the U.S. State Department proposed that the U.S. need not establish a stronghold in Vietnam to oppose Communist China's wider pattern of aggressive purposes. In their view, "a unified Communist Vietnam would reassert its traditional hostility to Communist China." This, in fact, is what came to pass when China and Vietnam eventually went to war in 1979 over the issue of Kampuchea.

In fact, going to war may cause a nation to suffer losses even when it is not defeated militarily. Battlefield victories are useful only if they lead to the establishment of a stable government. The lack of popular support for our allies in South Vietnam made such political control impossible. The United States thus lost prestige in Vietnam because, despite our superior military might, we lost the battle for the hearts and minds of the people. U.S. frustration led to the adoption of more brutal technologies of war—like napalm and chemical herbicides—that caused us to lose even more standing in the eyes of the world. Moreover, our own soldiers apparently suffered from the use of herbicides such as Agent Orange.

Because war puts the nation at such risk, the founders of our nation made certain that any such commitment would require a full public debate and declaration by Congress. In 1964, Presi-

116

dent Johnson used the little-understood Tonkin Gulf Resolution as a substitute for a declaration of war by Congress.

There were many negative consequences. First, Johnson was not free to mobilize all U.S. forces for a total commitment. Rather, he had to raise an army within the constraints of a peace-time Selective Service policy that allowed many of those from more prosperous families to escape service. The burden of the fighting was carried by lesser educated young men from poor white and minority families. Second, this deception contradicted a basic principle of our system: that citizens can influence important decisions through their elected representatives. This, in turn, provoked serious distrust in the political process and hostility toward U.S. leaders.

Many felt that the government plunged the country into war without adequate justification and without the consent of the public. Indeed, public opinion polls of the era bear this out. Although all U.S. presidents typically can assume a lot of public support, the American people were never convinced of the cause of Vietnam, and support for the war began to dwindle when casualties began to mount. From the beginning only about a third of the public had any confidence that South Vietnamese leaders would be able to establish a stable government, especially after U.S. troop withdrawal. Most Americans were concerned that we not provoke a wider war with China. Although hostile to a Communist takeover of Vietnam, most Americans were prepared to accept the Communists, if elected, as part of the government or to accept a neutral government, neither on the side of the United States nor the Communists. Most Americans supported bombing as a strategy but were opposed to the use of U.S. ground troops. Two of three wanted the burden of the fighting to be transferred to the South Vietnamese. In fact, the same proportion wanted to see the United Nations take over from the United States, either to fight or to settle the war.

These profound reservations about the war were much in evidence well before media coverage of the war turned critical. In fact, careful analysis of media coverage failed to turn up any evidence of bias against the military or the Nixon administration.

117

On the contrary, the Pentagon produced hundreds of propaganda films that were televised all over the nation, and the Johnson and Nixon administrations used censorship and the planting of false stories to mislead the press. Nevertheless, throughout the war the media gave the government the benefit of the doubt. This should not be surprising. Newspapers and television stations are giant corporations run by rich, white males who support big business. They make their profits by selling commercial time or space to other corporations. And they depend on government officials to help them make news. Three of four big city newspaper editors enthusiastically supported the war as late as 1967. And most television coverage of the war consisted of seventy-five- to ninety-second segments, usually based on official statements.

The smaller, alternative press generally did a better job than the mainstream press in going behind official government accounts to give Americans a more complete and accurate representation of events in Vietnam. In sum, the media reported on but certainly did not influence the decline in public support for the war.

Those who say we should have used even greater violence even earlier in the war need to ask themselves—for what purpose? How would U.S. national interests have been advanced by such a course? In addition, what greater risks would have been involved? Communist China and the Soviet Union provided North Vietnam with only a small fraction of the support that the United States provided South Vietnam. North Vietnam borders on China, and Soviet ships were docked in Haiphong Harbor. Would an invasion of the North or early mining of the harbor have forced China or the Soviet Union to become more involved?

Those who advocate unrestrained force should also know that all is never fair in war. For 2,500 years or more nations have worked to establish laws of warfare, addressing both the issues of adequate justification and proper conduct. These rules are practical as well as moral in purpose. By limiting casualties and preserving the spoils of war, they make it possible for leaders to choose war as a method of advancing their nation's interests. No winner wishes to destroy the other society, let alone wipe out all of its people. This would leave the victor with no subjects or wealth to exploit—in short, with no material gains.

It also should be understood that crimes against civilians were not only immoral but that they undermined the U.S. war effort by driving more and more neutrals into the ranks of the enemy. Certainly one can sympathize with the terror of U.S. soldiers not being able to distinguish friend from foe in a strange land ten thousand miles from home. However, even though humane treatment of civilians sometimes put a soldier's life at risk, it was his duty to remain civil in his dealings with the people.

A soldier's duty is not to stay alive by any means necessary. Such logic leads to combat avoidance, even desertion. A soldier's duty is to follow orders and be prepared to die if called upon. Such an order might be to charge a well-defended enemy position where many casualties can be predicted. Or it might be to not abuse civilians even if they might be suspected of collaborating with the enemy. Again, soldiers who showed no discipline and violated the military code by abusing Vietnamese civilians only increased the size and determination of the opposing forces.

In the final analysis, these issues of political process and public opinion are central to understanding our failed policy in Vietnam. War is more than a contest of troops and technology. It is a struggle between nations, and it has economic, cultural, social, and political, as well as military, dimensions.

When people believe in a cause, they are capable of extraordinary sacrifices; and soldiers are capable of extraordinary courage. The Communists in Vietnam were inspired by the vision of an independent, unified nation and able to rally people to their cause. They persisted despite twice the per capita battle death rate as Japan had in World War II. In South Vietnam, on the other hand, the government, its military, and its U.S. allies had too little public support. Many perceived them as holdovers from French colonial days or as defenders of wealth and privilege. Only one of ten U.S. generals who commanded in Vietnam saw the Army of the Republic of (South) Vietnam as "an acceptable fighting force," and over half said the war either "had not been worth it or should not have progressed beyond an advisory effort."

Clearly, the American public needs a cause it can believe in before it sends its sons off to war, and that cause must be solidly based in clearly stated national principle and interest. American power is not infinite. It must be exercised with great care and only where our vital national interests are at stake. Few today believe that Vietnam ever qualified by these standards.

James Stockdale

Admiral, U.S. Navy, retired; Senior Naval Service Prisoner of War, Hanoi, 1965–73

First, we lost it. Second, we could have won it. We could have won it easily if from the start we had fought the real enemy, North Vietnam. Instead we assumed that the enemy was the South Vietnamese insurgents, the Viet Cong, and we wasted all our energy on them. They were merely cannon fodder, doing whatever the North Vietnamese told them to do to wear us down.

Third, the real enemy, North Vietnam, could easily have been made to surrender and cease making trouble in South Vietnam if we had attacked the North Vietnamese capital city, Hanoi, with bombs, from the start. I know this to be true because I spent most of the war as a prisoner in Hanoi. I watched the North Vietnamese people's reaction to the bombs. I knew from talking to the prison commissar that they were laughing up their sleeves at our halfhearted efforts in the North and at our misdirected loss of men in the South. When America finally brought the B-52s into the Hanoi area and conducted concentrated bombings in late 1972, the North Vietnamese surrendered. They would have surrendered in just the same way if we had brought B-52s in and bombed the same way the day the war started, eight years before. With our precision delivery methods, the casualties to the North Vietnamese would have been very light (as they were in 1972), and 58,000 American lives would have been spared.

Fourth, the reason our government chose to settle for half-hearted, self-defeating moves in the Vietnam War was its lack of trust in the American people's judgment. Our political leaders knew they could not bomb Hanoi unless they could convince middle America that their aims in committing force to Vietnam were sound. Their lack of confidence in the people's judgment brought about an undeclared war, fought on the sly, without any comprehensive, meaningful explanation to the soldiers or to their fathers and mothers.

Fifth, junior high school students should realize that the founding fathers were correct in writing into the Constitution the provision that only the Congress, only the people, can declare war. If the people don't understand a war, if they don't support it, our armed conflict will degenerate into halfhearted, deceptive measures. These usually spell defeat.

And sixth, students should know that soldiers don't decide on wars. They just follow orders and fight them. And in Vietnam, our soldiers fought bravely and well.

Thanks for being a schoolteacher. My four sons do the same.

Oliver Stone

Infantryman, U.S. Army, Vietnam, 1967–68; writer, director of the motion picture *Platoon*

When Lyndon Johnson pulled out in March, 1968, the war was metaphorically over. The grunts sensed it right away. We were never going to win, but we had to withdraw with a semblance of dignity. That semblance of dignity took four more years of deceit and death, and, in the moral vacuum, there was never any clear reason to us why we should die. Dissension and mutiny grew in the ranks between draftees and officers and lifer sergeants. Fraggings on a scale never seen in modern war occurred, and black/white relations grew worse with the assassination of Martin Luther King, Jr. Marijuana, and eventually heroin, usage engulfed a portion of the troops.

The ultimate corruption was, of course, President Johnson sending only the poor and uneducated to the war—in fact practicing class warfare wherein the middle and upper classes could avoid the war by going to college or paying a psychiatrist. I am sure to this day that if the middle and upper classes had gone to Vietnam, their mothers and fathers (the politicians and businessmen) would have ended that war a hell of a lot sooner; in fact, politicians' sons, if not politicians themselves, should be sent to every war first.

I think that ultimately we were destined to lose the war even before we started, or to paraphrase Sun Tzu, "every war is won before it is ever fought." We were destined to lose because the Vietnam War had no moral purpose, and it was fought without any moral integrity. And we did lose, because, basically, as a character in *Platoon* says, "we were not the good guys anymore."

Mary Stout

Army Nurse Corps, Vietnam, 1966–67;
President, Vietnam Veterans of America

My years of advocacy on behalf of veterans have given me some interesting perspectives on what we should teach our children about the Vietnam War.

Vietnam veterans' views on the war differ little from the opinions of the general public—opinion surveys have shown that Vietnam veterans, like the nation at large, are evenly split over the question whether the war was right or wrong. While I have personally come to believe that the war was a mistake, I also believe that neither the "rightness" of the war nor the question who is responsible for our defeat are the most important lessons we can learn from the war.

The single most important lesson that I would like to see passed along to future generations is the tragic mistake we have made as a nation in tying our feelings about the war to our treatment of the men and women who served in that war.

Now, years later, the American people have come to realize that you can support the warrior even while disagreeing about the war. (As usual, the government has not kept pace with its citizens, but I am hopeful that we will soon begin to see Vietnam veterans finally getting their due in terms of government programs and support.)

However, for far too many years the American people, in their attempt to forget about the awful experience of Vietnam, closed themselves off from all reminders of the war, including the men and women who sacrificed for their country.

Despite the attempts of a few revisionist historians, this inexcusable behavior cannot be ascribed to one political group or another. For different reasons both conservatives and liberals were equally guilty of turning their backs on their fellow Americans who had served their country.

If I can use my current position to make one contribution to history, I would like it to be in the area of respect for serving one's country. I look forward to the day when our society readily grants recognition and assistance to the men and women who fought for our nation, without stopping to debate whether a war was right or wrong, or whether politicians or the military were to blame for a military loss. America's debt to our warriors should be based solely on the issue of service to one's country.

Harry G. Summers, Jr.

Editor, *Vietnam* magazine; author of *On Strategy: A Critical Analysis of the Vietnam War* and *Vietnam War Almanac*

I would emphasize three factors:

1. Since most students have no knowledge whatsoever of civics, I would emphasize that war is a political act and the military only the instrument. A series of presidents from Truman through Ford ordered the military into action, and a series of Congresses from 1950 to 1973 appropriated the necessary funds for the prosecution of the war.

2. Because it was a political act, the failure to mobilize public support proved fatal. Americans don't fight wars in cold blood, and it was a mistake to order American troops into sustained combat without first obtaining a declaration of war from the Congress—the "representatives of the people, periodically elected."

3. Like the war itself, the failure was political—the inability of our senior civilian and military officials to devise a strategy worthy of the name. America's soldiers, sailors, airmen, and marines withdrew from Vietnam during the period 1969–73 not because they were forced out by the Viet Cong or North Vietnamese but because they were ordered out for domestic political reasons. All American military forces had left Vietnam by January, 1973, over two years before Saigon fell to the North Vietnamese twenty-two-division–cross-border blitzkrieg.

Sherry Svoboda

Concerned citizen; mother; housewife

I was a fourth grader at Tyndall Elementary School, at Tyndall Air Force Base, Florida. I can recall that it was a pretty, crisp fall day only a few weeks into the school year. My teacher, Miss Call, was wearing a dress with a lovely fall floral pattern. I had asked to go to the restroom and was just returning to the classroom when I saw Miss Call speaking to the principal outside our classroom. Miss Call had tears rolling down her cheeks. This scared the life out of me. I had never seen a teacher cry before.

I reentered the classroom and took my seat. Moments later Miss Call reentered the room. She had regained her composure. "Karen," she said, "please collect your personal items and go to the front office. Your mother will meet you there."

After Karen had left, Miss Call informed the class that Karen's father had been reported Missing in Action in Vietnam. I never saw Karen again. One of the other children in class who lived near Karen's family reported to the class a few days later that Karen and her family had moved from their Base Housing. I didn't really grasp what "Missing in Action" meant, only that in my limited view it meant that we would never see or hear from Karen again.

This scenario was repeated probably a half dozen times over the next two years. We never saw any of those children again, and I have never learned of the fate of their fathers.

Soon, my father began wearing a button that had an "Unhappy Face" with the slogan "POWs Never Have A Nice Day." When I asked him what a POW was my father told me about the men who had been captured by the North Vietnamese. So that I would understand the concept, he brought home articles and photographs that showed the prison camps and conditions under which the American soldiers who were POWs lived. I can remember him telling me that the fathers of the children in my classes were either dead or were POWs.

125

Because of his work with experimental missiles, my father was never required to go to Vietnam. He told me that the work he was doing at Tyndall was very important to our country's abilities to maintain its position as a world power, and he assured me that he would never be sent to Vietnam. This explanation failed to calm my subconscious fears, and I had recurring nightmares of being told to meet my mother in the principal's office.

Another memory that comes to mind takes place a few years after the first. One day a group of children from our neighborhood had gathered on our screened porch. It was a rainy, late-summer day. Nixon was campaigning for president with promises to end the Vietnam War if he were elected. We all decided to "vote" for Nixon, because that meant, to us at least, that no more children would lose their fathers.

I, as a parent, can only pray that my son never looks back on childhood memories and finds anything of the sort that I do. I hope that you succeed in determining how to teach the present and future generations about the war in Vietnam. Maybe you could also teach them a little bit about how precious peace is.

Howard N. Tanner

Air Force fighter pilot in World War II, Korea, and Vietnam

There are so many facets relative to the conflict in Vietnam that all the books written about Vietnam have not been able to cover all of them.

One of the little-known factors affecting the Vietnam operation is the understanding of shipping lanes and "strategic choke points." Maritime shipping is vital to every country in the world, and this was forcibly brought to everyone's attention during World War II, when Germany attempted to interdict the shipping lanes of Great Britain and the Soviet Union while the Japanese were attacking the shipping lanes of the United States. The number of choke points will vary depending on an individual's evaluation of the strategic areas in the world, but I believe most experts will agree with the following list: Suez Canal, Gibraltar, Cape of Good Hope, Panama Canal, Cape Horn, Singapore, and South Vietnam. Understandably, the troubled spots in our world today include nearly every one of these strategic choke points, because the country controlling these choke points can control world shipping.

Historians note that there have been dissenters against every war in which we have been involved. I remember the actions of protestors during World War II and Korea, but during those periods their actions were effectively curbed. The difference during the Vietnam War was that the protestors received support from government officials. Robert S. McNamara has admitted that he advised the president *many times* that the United States could not win in Vietnam! This statement came from the man who *totally* controlled the military operations in Vietnam. If he did not completely believe in the duties assigned to him, he should have turned control over to someone willing to do what was required of him instead of sitting in Washington, D.C., sacrificing more than 58,000 American lives! Vietnam war protestors had to have governmental support to be able to travel to an enemy country, make unfounded, treasonable statements against our country and fighting men, and do so with impunity!

God knows that investigative reporters for the media have investigated nearly everything under the sun! Why have no reports ever been presented to the American public on those who profited from the contracts let to civilian firms doing U.S. government work in Vietnam? Why has the media continued to remain silent on how the Soviet Union's bureau of misinformation duped the Western media into believing the Tet Offensive was a great victory for Vietnam? The time for *all* the "unvarnished truth" has long since passed! When will the American people be allowed to understand that as a result of this tragic fiasco, untold millions of South Vietnamese and Cambodians have been killed and/or imprisoned by the North Vietnamese?

Telford Taylor

Lawyer; writer; author of
Nuremberg and Vietnam

Far more important for students than considering the military actions and the eventual ending of the war is an awareness of the process by which the United States became involved in the war. The contrast between that story and the road to participation in our other twentieth-century wars is very marked and shows how a sequence of decisions at high executive level, unsupported by full public understanding, can lead to a situation in which withdrawal is very difficult, public support is shakey and lessening, and public and political tensions are created that threaten democratic government.

Garry Trudeau

Creator of the comic strip *Doonesbury*

The most important thing for today's students to understand about the Vietnam War is that while their country entered into the war for moral reasons, it also got out for moral reasons.

William Tuohy

Vietnam correspondent, *Los Angeles Times*, 1966–68

The most important thing for your students to understand about the Vietnam War is the limitation on the use of American power abroad. That is to say that while the United States is a nuclear-armed superpower, it found that such power could not be appropriately deployed in Vietnam.

From this follows the corollary that the United States should not commit itself to using force, as in Vietnam, unless that military power can be used successfully.

I leave it to the historians to determine whether the U.S. involvement was moral or not, but I think it is now clear that we were not able to deploy our military might successfully against the Viet Cong and the North Vietnamese, who used military forces with much less firepower but with more effectiveness.

The Vietnamese experience also shows that the American public is incapable of supporting a long, drawn-out struggle involving U.S. troops—but that without such support any major overseas commitment is probably doomed to failure.

Kurt Vonnegut

Novelist; author of *Slaughterhouse Five* and *Cat's Cradle*

One of the most important things to learn in school is that movies lie about deaths from gunshot if they show them to be instantaneous and free of gore, if they make them seem almost fun.

John Waghelstein

Served two tours in Vietnam; Commander, 7th Special Forces Group, Fort Bragg, North Carolina

Students should be made aware that in Vietnam:

1. Our desire was to help a friend in need, and we hoped for a democratic Vietnam. These hopes were noble and consistent with our ideals as a nation.

2. We learned that the United States alone cannot win another country's war, no matter how noble. The leaders of the other country must be willing to erase the causes of the discontent that allow guerrilla movements to take hold. In Vietnam these issues were land reform, unjust taxation, the draft, and foreign presence.

3. We learned that military force is no substitute for political, social, and economic action. The South Vietnamese government could not or would not make the necessary changes.

4. We *relearned* that the American public is impatient with protracted war when our own vital interests are not clearly stated and readily apparent. Vietnam was too far away to be important to most Americans.

5. We learned that the United States, by focusing on a military victory, could not win when the other parts of the equation were ignored.

Frank Walker

Tactical interrogator, 11th Armored Cavalry
Regiment, Vietnam and Cambodia, 1969–70

I have an eleven-year-old son who is forming questions about Vietnam but has yet to ask them. He and my daughter, who knows nothing of Vietnam, live with their mother. We all live in the suburbs of Washington, D.C. A few months ago my son and I were spending the day at the Mall. I took him to the Vietnam Memorial, because I am always drawn to it when I am near. When the tears came to my eyes, he wanted to ask some of the questions, but he knew that I could not answer. He still hasn't asked, but someday soon he will. I want to answer your question to help me articulate what I must one day say to my son and my daughter.

Why did we lose the war? We were fighting two separate wars over there. First, we were involved in a civil war within the country of South Vietnam—the Saigon government against the Viet Cong. Second, we were fighting an invading army from another country. Forget that the two countries shared part of their names. They *were* separate countries. At no other time has the United States had to fight such a two-pronged war. Regardless of our intentions or qualifications as a fighting force, that fact doomed us from the beginning. Both were formidable enemies. If we had taken the war to the North, we would have lost in the South. We fought in the South and lost to the North.

I was a tactical interrogator at squadron level in the 11th Armored Cavalry Regiment in Vietnam and Cambodia. I interrogated North Vietnamese regulars and Viet Cong prisoners over ten months in the field.

Most North Vietnamese prisoners were young (most were only teenagers, barely older than your junior high school students), inexperienced, and scared. One had never seen an American before being captured. He had been told that we were all big, ugly, hairy monsters with fangs instead of teeth. Most of the prisoners I talked to had just come down the Ho Chi Minh Trail through Cambodia into South Vietnam. Perhaps later, if they survived, they became more hardcore, but when I saw them they were much like us—only younger. They had the advantage of youth and numbers.

Most of the Viet Cong prisoners I interrogated were older—usually in their thirties or forties. They and their families had been fighting for years—beginning with the French. They were no happier under the Saigon government than they were under the French. To them, they were continuing to fight social and political inequities. They had the advantage of commitment. They were not fighting because they were told to; they were fighting for their country and a way of life. They were totally dedicated to their beliefs.

I was a good interrogator, but I could get nowhere with Viet Cong prisoners. They had been interrogated by countless like me before and would be again before we withdrew four years later. I also knew that in a few days each of them would be free to once again wage their war against us and Saigon.

As soldiers fighting a war, we witnessed the horrors of war, but none that weren't witnessed by our fathers and grandfathers in other wars. What was different about this one? Why have so many of us become victims of Delayed Stress Syndrome? That is the question I have to answer for myself before I can pass it along to my children. Maybe it was because of the two wars we were fighting. Do we see ourselves in the same position as Germany did in occupied European countries? Do we see ourselves as the bad guys?

Were we so far apart from the Vietnamese people—socially, politically, economically, culturally—that we came to hate all of them and see all of them as the enemy?

Our lack of clarity made us as individuals do things we would not have thought ourselves capable of doing. War crimes? Yes, we committed war crimes. War itself is a crime. With victory, however, comes justification and absolution. We had no victory, and there are no indulgences for our crimes. Perhaps that is the burden that we must carry.

I know that I have not answered any of the questions of your students or my son or myself. Perhaps I have, in writing this, forced myself to ask even more questions. But this is something that we all must do if we are to understand the Vietnam experience.

Paul C. Warnke

General Counsel, Department of Defense, 1966–67; Assistant Secretary of Defense for International Security Affairs, 1967–69; Chief U.S. Negotiator, SALT, 1977–78

To me the most important thing to understand about the Vietnam War is that it was not a military defeat. We could have continued indefinitely a military occupation of South Vietnam that would have prevented the North Vietnamese from taking over the entire country. To do so, however, would have meant continued immense human, social, and financial expenditure with no conclusive victory in sight.

The fact is that the government of Vietnam, in Saigon, was an artificial contrivance that enjoyed no significant popular support. The nationalist drive was centered in Hanoi and the Viet Cong. We became involved because we viewed the Indochinese conflict as part of a global struggle with the Soviet Union and the People's Republic of China. It was, instead, an indigenous revolution in which we had no legitimate role.

It is, of course, much easier to reach these conclusions now than it was in the early 1960s, when we regarded Russia and China as a Communist monolith and feared Chinese domination of the entire Far East.

James H. Webb, Jr.

Vietnam veteran; Assistant Secretary of Defense, 1984–87; Secretary of the Navy, 1987–88; author of *Fields of Fire*

I believe that today's young people should understand that Vietnam was a war of good intentions, with important issues at stake: issues of national commitment, of freedom from oppression in the same sense that the Korean War involved those issues, and issues of global security, which became more clear after the war was lost. But it was a war where our national goals were never clearly articulated by the Johnson administration, and where, as a result, the forces we deployed were not structured or deployed toward a definite end. Time went on, lives were lost, and the public finally despaired of an inconclusive and costly commitment.

Caspar W. Weinberger

U.S. Secretary of Defense, 1981–87

I believe the post-Vietnam period has taught us several lessons, and from them I have developed six major tests to be applied when we are weighing the use of U.S. combat forces abroad.

First, the United States should not commit forces to combat overseas unless the particular engagement or occasion is deemed vital to our national interest or that of our allies. That emphatically does not mean that we should declare beforehand, as we did with Korea in 1950, that a particular area is outside our strategic perimeter.

Second, if we decide it is necessary to put combat troops into a given situation, we should do so wholeheartedly, and with the clear intention of winning. If we are unwilling to commit the forces or resources necessary to achieve our objectives, we should not commit them at all. Of course, if the particular situation requires only limited force to win our objectives, then we should not hesitate to commit forces sized accordingly. When Hitler broke treaties and remilitarized the Rhineland, small combat forces then could perhaps have prevented the Holocaust of World War II.

Third, if we do decide to commit forces to combat overseas, we should have clearly defined political and military objectives. And we should know precisely how our forces can accomplish those clearly defined objectives. And we should have, and send, the forces needed to do just that. As Karl von Clausewitz wrote, "No one starts a war—or, rather, no one in his senses ought to do so—without first being clear in his mind what he intends to achieve by that war, and how he intends to conduct it."

War may be different today than it was in Clausewitz's time, but the need for well-defined objectives and a consistent strategy is still essential. If we determine that a combat mission has become necessary for our vital national interests, then we must send forces capable to do the job—and not assign a combat mission to a force configured for peacekeeping.

Fourth, the relationship between our objectives and the forces we have committed—their size, composition, and disposition—must be continually reassessed and adjusted if necessary. Conditions and objectives invariably change during the course of a conflict. When they do change, then so must our combat requirements. We must continuously keep as a beacon before us the basic questions: Is this conflict in our national interest? Does our national interest require us to fight, to use force of arms? If the answers are *yes*, then we must win. If the answers are *no*, then we should not be in combat.

Fifth, before the U.S. commits combat forces abroad, there must be some reasonable assurance that we will have the support of the American people and their elected representatives in Congress. This support cannot be achieved unless we are candid in making clear the threats we face; the support cannot be sustained without continued and close consultation. We cannot fight a battle with the Congress at home while asking our troops to win a war overseas or, as in the case of Vietnam, in effect asking our troops not to win, but just to be there.

Finally, the commitment of U.S. forces to combat should be a last resort.

Spencer Welch

Concerned citizen

Bill McCloud's eighth graders could probably teach him a lesson about war, for they are the first generation in all history brought up to truly reject war, to reject it absolutely as an option. This rejection is so total and clear that it has become "self-evident," so agreed upon that it simply isn't discussed any more.

Barbara Tuchman maintains that if society had seen television pictures of the battles of World War I every night over soup and supper, the war would have stopped by popular demand. If so, World War II probably would not have occurred, or if it had, we might have stopped Hitler earlier. The point is that communications have already started to produce a "global village" consciousness . . . at least in the West. As part of this development, most of us simply won't put up with butchery in our living rooms.

That this is a heartening development is truly self-evident. But the lessons to be learned are profound and vital. Profound in that they teach us that society's values are essentially positive: given real choices, we will usually opt for life, health, and hope. Vital in that children must see that every generation from now on must guard its right to know and see, to fight censorship.

136

The press was banned from Grenada, and Henry Kissinger advised Israel to keep them out of Palestine. Both actions blurred our understanding of two important conflicts, blunting the sheer ridiculous nature of the first and the ongoing vicious injustice of the second. Of course, the press is also barred from South Africa and from much of the Communist world, with continuing distortions, half-truths, and confusion as a result.

Any course on the lessons of the Vietnam War should include consideration of the following questions: (1) What forces and techniques created the age-old vision of war as glorious, manly, character-building, etc., when it is so obviously a horror? (2) What forces in society benefited from this vision, from war itself, and how did they bring these about? (3) Who fought and got butchered and maimed, and who directed, planned, and financed war? And finally, (4) How do we guard our rights to see and to know?

William C. Westmoreland

Commander, U.S. Military Assistance Command, Vietnam, 1964–68; Chief of Staff, U.S. Army, 1968–72

The Vietnam War was a limited war, with limited objectives, prosecuted by limited means, with limited public support. Therefore, it was destined to be (and was) a long war, a war so long that public support waned and political decisions by the Congress terminated our involvement, resulting in a military victory by the North Vietnamese Communists following the withdrawal of American combat troops.

The military did not lose a single battle of consequence and did not lose the war. The war was lost by congressional actions withdrawing support to the South Vietnamese government despite commitments by President Nixon.

Robert Wilson

Book editor, *USA Today*

I think it is essential for students to understand the way in which the war developed: incrementally and, I believe, illegally. Had the people understood what kind of war we were getting into, and, indeed, if they had realized that we were getting into any kind of war, they surely would not have permitted it. Because the executive branch of the government arrogated power that the legislative branch should not have given up, the government was first able to mislead the people and then ignore them. Congress should have ended the war many years before it did.

I also think that it is important for students to understand the truths about any war, that war is brutal and dehumanizing to those who fight it, that many of its costs are hidden and that its ill effects can last for generations, that it is an outrage to romanticize war in any way or to pretend that it is something that it is not.

Ronald L. Ziegler

Press Secretary and Assistant to President Nixon, 1969–74

In our Republic, a military engagement cannot be conducted unless the commander-in-chief, the president, has the support of the American people and/or the ability to stimulate support for the efforts.

The ultimate tragedy of the Vietnam experience occurred because the government could not maintain the support it needed. The American people could not, in the long term, justify U.S.

involvement. While the presidency—and our government system—is fully accountable to the forces of public opinion, a president must not formulate decisions solely on the pressures of public opinion.

The president absolutely must have the capacity to rally public opinion to support his policies.

The bottom line is: Vietnam showed us the power of citizen involvement in a situation that brought the United States a great deal of criticism from its allies and from within. Vietnam also taught us a lesson that should inspire young people: It is important to be educated, informed, and involved.

E. R. Zumwalt, Jr.

Commander, U.S. Naval Forces, Vietnam, 1968–70; Chief of Naval Operations, 1970–74

The most important thing for young people to recognize is the immense challenge to our democratic way of life as this globe struggles to adapt to burgeoning populations, polluting environments, and dwindling resources. And all in a world in which there is no overall rule of law.

Afterword

W hat should we tell our children about Vietnam? That may end up being the question that won't go away. I think that, at best, there is no definitive answer.

The importance of this collection is that it puts into the hands of teachers, parents, and students answers to that question from a wide variety of people—people who had some stake in the conflict at the time and still carry strong feelings about it today.

Now when young people ask us about Vietnam, and especially the lessons to be learned, we have something specific from which to form an answer.

I do not encourage teachers specifically to teach any one of the lessons found throughout this book. It is up to each individual to decide which of the lessons he or she thinks should be taught. My main hope is that this book will encourage more adults of the Vietnam generation to begin talking about the war with today's young people.

Having said that, I can note some of the lessons that are mentioned most frequently. I will also point out, however, that even on these points, agreement would not be unanimous.

The lessons include:

1. We learned again the grimness of war, and students need to understand that war is not the way it has been traditionally portrayed in the movies and on television, where it often seems glamorous, maybe even fun.

2. Our cause was just, maybe even noble, because we entered the war for moral, unselfish reasons.

3. The United States went into Vietnam to stop the spread of communism.

4. The United States never fielded better armies. The American military performance was outstanding, and our soldiers fought bravely and well.

5. Nevertheless, the war was probably a mistake.

6. The United States should never engage in a war not formally declared by Congress.

7. The United States should not intervene in another country with military force unless that country is a serious threat to our own security.

8. We must not engage in war without a total commitment to win.

9. The United States learned that there are limits to its power in a nuclear age.

10. We went into Vietnam thinking that it was a battle between us and the Communist bloc—but we discovered that communism is not the same in every country, and that the Vietnamese were fighting for the survival of their own country. We overestimated the closeness of the Soviet Union and China to North Vietnam—and underestimated the determination of the North Vietnamese.

11. The United States ended up fighting an "unwinnable war" because of (a) the broad popular support for the Viet Cong, (b) the corruption of the South Vietnamese government, and (c) the limits the United States imposed upon itself (i.e., not to invade North Vietnam, not to use nuclear weapons, not to invade neighboring countries to destroy the Ho Chi Minh Trail, not to bomb the airfield at Hanoi for fear of killing a Soviet or Chinese citizen, not to overthrow Ho Chi Minh, etc.).

12. All wars are an enormous waste of life. All wars are failures because it means the leaders on both sides have failed to resolve their differences by peaceful and civilized means.

13. Citizens of all ages need to stay informed about world affairs and what our government is doing.

The time has come for all Americans to face squarely the matter of the lessons of the Vietnam War. As several of my contributors have noted, the American people must share in any blame associated with the war, and it is the responsibility of the American people to see that any mistakes that were made are not repeated.

A good starting point would be for every American to read the letters in this book. Then let's use the outpouring of hindsight, reflection, sorrow, anger, remorse, pride, and defiance found in these letters to begin talking to our children about the Vietnam War. They want to know about it. They should know about it. And so many of us have a need to talk about it.

The time has come.

Chronology

1954

After the last major engagement of the French Indochina War, French forces surrender to the nationalist Viet Minh troops at Dien Bien Phu, Vietnam.

Peace talks at the Geneva Conference end with the issuance of a final declaration establishing a temporary military demarcation line dividing Vietnam until a political settlement can be achieved through nationwide elections. The elections are never held.

1955

U.S. advisers replace the French in training the South Vietnamese Army.

The Republic of Vietnam is proclaimed, with Ngo Dinh Diem its president.

1956

The U.S. Military Assistance Advisory Group (MAAG) officially takes over from the departing French the responsibility for training the Army of the Republic of Vietnam (ARVN).

1959

Two U.S. military advisers become the first Americans killed in the Vietnam War, when Viet Cong forces attack the air base at Bien Hoa.

145

1962

The American Military Assistance Command, Vietnam (MACV) is formed in South Vietnam, as the United States reorganizes its military command there. From this time on the conduct of the war is directed by MACV, which supervises MAAG.

1963

South Vietnam's President Ngo Dinh Diem is killed during a military coup.

1964

North Vietnamese PT boats fire torpedoes at the U.S. destroyer *Maddox* in the Gulf of Tonkin.

The U.S. House and Senate overwhelmingly approve the Gulf of Tonkin Resolution, granting presidential authority to order retaliatory attacks in Vietnam.

The first Congressional Medal of Honor of the Vietnam War is awarded to U.S. Army Captain Roger Donlon.

Two Americans die in a bombing of the U.S. Officers' Quarters in Saigon.

1965

Buddhists begin demonstrations in South Vietnam against the South Vietnamese military government, because they claim it is being kept in power by the Americans.

A Viet Cong attack on the U.S. base at Pleiku results in eight U.S. servicemen being killed.

The sustained American bombing of North Vietnam (Operation Rolling Thunder) begins.

The first American ground combat troops arrive in Da Nang, South Vietnam.

The University of Michigan holds the first "teach-in" on Vietnam; during the next two months teach-ins on Vietnam are held on more than one hundred American college campuses.

The first mass bombing raid in Vietnam takes place as B-52s attack a Viet Cong concentration thirty miles north of Saigon.

American forces defeat North Vietnamese units in the Ia Drang Valley in the first major conventional clash of the war.

The Defense Department issues the largest draft call since the Korean War.

Antiwar demonstrations occur in more than thirty American cities, the largest involving twenty thousand people in Washington, D.C.

1966

There are scenes of antiwar protest at graduation exercises throughout the month of June on several American college campuses.

The United States ends its policy of avoiding major North Vietnamese cities in bombing raids, as American planes attack oil installations, highways, and bridges in Hanoi and Haiphong.

Military officials announce that U.S. planes have begun defoliating huge areas of jungle to destroy cover used by Communist troops.

1967

Massive antiwar demonstrations occur throughout the United States, especially in New York City and Washington, D.C.

1968

Communists launch the massive Tet offensive on Saigon and most other major cities and provincial capitals of South Vietnam.

President Johnson announces that he has called for an immediate halt to the bombing of North Vietnam above the 20th parallel and that he will not seek reelection.

Students seize several buildings at Columbia University and occupy President Grayson Kirk's offices to begin a week-long takeover of the university in protest of, among other things, the war in Vietnam.

The Vietnam War becomes the longest war in American history.

Chicago is the scene of the most violent national party convention in American history, as antiwar demonstrators clash with police at the Democratic National Convention.

President Johnson announces a complete halt to all American bombing of North Vietnam.

1969

Discussions begin in earnest at the Vietnam War Peace Talks in Paris, after weeks of debate have finally established the shape of the negotiating table.

President Nixon orders the secret bombing of Cambodia.

U.S. combat deaths in Vietnam surpass the number killed in the Korean War (33,629).

U.S. troop strength in Vietnam reaches its peak of 543,400.

North Vietnamese leader Ho Chi Minh dies.

The trial of the "Chicago 8" begins; the defendants are radical leaders of the protestors during the Democratic Convention, accused of conspiring to incite a riot.

Massive antiwar demonstrations occur throughout the United States; one in Washington, D.C., involves more than 200,000 people.

Seymour Hersh breaks the story that more than four hundred villagers had been massacred by American soldiers at My Lai on March 16, 1968; the army begins an investigation.

President Nixon signs a bill allowing for a lottery for Selective Service draftees.

President Nixon announces a withdrawal of 50,000 U.S. troops from Vietnam, the third reduction since he took office.

1970

The defendants in the Chicago 8 trial are acquitted of charges of conspiring to incite a riot at the 1968 Democratic National Convention; convictions on lesser charges are later overturned.

President Nixon announces he will bring 150,000 troops home from Vietnam by the spring of 1971.

President Nixon announces that U.S. troops have crossed into Cambodia to destroy Communist sanctuaries and supply bases.

National Guardsmen fire into a crowd of students protesting the war at Kent State University, in Ohio, killing four students and wounding nine.

More than two hundred U.S. colleges close down, and huge crowds gather in major American cities to protest the expansion of the war into Cambodia and the killing of the students at Kent State.

State and city police open fire on demonstrators at Jackson State College, in Mississippi; two students are killed.

The U.S. Senate votes to repeal the Gulf of Tonkin Resolution.

The U.S. withdraws all forces from Cambodia.

The U.S. Senate passes the Cooper-Church Amendment, barring U.S. military personnel from Cambodia.

The White House announces a phaseout of defoliation operations in Vietnam.

1971

Lt. William Calley is convicted of murder for his part in the My Lai massacre; he is sentenced to life in prison, later reduced to twenty years.

President Nixon announces that 100,000 additional U.S. troops will be withdrawn from Vietnam by the end of the year.

Two major antiwar demonstrations take place in Washington, D.C., one resulting in the arrest of ten thousand people.

The *New York Times* begins publication of the Pentagon Papers.

President Nixon announces new troop reductions, to leave 139,000 there by February of 1972, and states that the U.S. ground combat role has ended.

The U.S. conducts massive sustained air attacks on military targets in North Vietnam.

1972

President Nixon announces U.S. troop levels in Vietnam will be decreased to 69,000 by May 1.

President Nixon reveals that National Security Adviser Henry Kissinger has been involved in secret peace talks in Paris with Le Duc Tho of the Hanoi Politburo.

The last U.S. ground combat troops leave Vietnam; 43,500 service personnel, pilots, and advisers remain.

President Nixon announces the military draft will end by mid-1973.

Henry Kissinger announces that "peace is at hand" in Vietnam; Radio Hanoi announces a breakthrough in the peace talks.

The Paris Peace Talks end without an agreement.

President Nixon orders the resumption of full-scale bombing in Vietnam.

1973

Kissinger and Le Duc Tho resume talks in Paris after the bombing of Vietnam is halted above the twentieth parallel.

Citing progress in the peace talks, President Nixon announces the end of all hostile actions against North Vietnam.

President Nixon announces an agreement for "peace with honor" in Vietnam.

The American involvement in Vietnam officially ends with the formal signing of the cease-fire agreement.

American POWs are released from captivity in North Vietnam.

The last American troops leave South Vietnam.

150

Congress overrides President Nixon's veto of the War Powers Act, a law limiting the President's right to wage war.

1974

The House of Representatives rejects the Nixon administration's request for an increase in military aid to South Vietnam.

The conviction of Lieutenant Calley is overturned because of prejudicial pretrial publicity.

1975

The North Vietnamese Army opens an offensive against South Vietnam and in less than a month takes control of major coastal cities.

The Senate Armed Services Committee rejects President Ford's request for additional emergency aid for South Vietnam.

South Vietnam surrenders to the Viet Cong and other Communist forces as Saigon falls.

The U.S. freighter *Mayaguez* is seized by Cambodian Communists.

The forty-man crew of the *Mayaguez* is released unharmed; forty-two U.S. would-be rescuers died during the incident.

1977

President Carter pardons most of the ten thousand Vietnam War draft evaders.

Vietnam is admitted to the United Nations.

1979

The U.S. General Accounting Office reports, despite previous denials by the defense department, that thousands of U.S. troops were exposed to the toxic defoliant Agent Orange while serving in Vietnam.

1982

The Vietnam Veterans Memorial is dedicated in Washington, D.C.

1984

Federal District Judge Jack B. Weinstein announces a $170 million out-of-court settlement against seven chemical companies in a class-action suit brought by a group of Vietnam veterans against manufacturers of the defoliant Agent Orange.

The only American Unknown Soldier from the Vietnam War is laid to rest during ceremonies at Arlington National Cemetery, in Washington, D.C.

A statue of three Vietnam War servicemen is dedicated at the Vietnam Veterans Memorial in Washington, D.C.

1989

After the end of all legal challenges, the first payments from the Agent Orange settlement fund are made to families of 172 Vietnam veterans whose deaths were linked to the defoliant.

Suggested Readings

The following books are appropriate (and recommended) for use with junior high school students in the classroom:

Bender, David L. *The Vietnam War: Opposing Viewpoints.* St. Paul, Minn.: Greenhaven Press, 1984.

Fincher, E. B. *The Vietnam War.* New York: Franklin Watts, 1980.

The Illustrated History of the Vietnam War. New York: Bantam Books, 1987–88.

Vol. 1   *Marines,* by Edwin H. Simmons
Vol. 2   *Sky Soldiers,* by F. Clifton Berry, Jr.
Vol. 3   *Armor,* by James R. Arnold
Vol. 4   *Carrier Operations,* by Edward J. Marolda
Vol. 5   *Khe Sanh,* by Michael Ewing
Vol. 6   *Tunnel Warfare,* by Tom Mangold and John Penycate
Vol. 7   *Artillery,* by James R. Arnold
Vol. 8   *Riverine Force,* by John Forbes and Bob Williams
Vol. 9   *Strike Aircraft,* by F. Clifton Berry, Jr.
Vol. 10   *Rangers,* by James R. Arnold
Vol. 11   *Helicopters,* by John Guilmartin, Jr., and Michael O'Leary
Vol. 12   *Chargers,* by F. Clifton Berry, Jr.

Katcher, Philip. *Armies of the Vietnam War, 1962–75.* London: Osprey, 1980.

Lawson, Don. *An Album of the Vietnam War.* New York: Franklin Watts, 1986.

———. *The War in Vietnam.* New York: Franklin Watts, 1981.

Mabie, Margot C. J. *Vietnam: There and Here.* New York: Henry Holt, 1985.

The Vietnam Experience. 20 vols. Boston: Boston Publishing, 1987.

The following books are recommended for background reading and as reference works for teachers:

Asia Society, The. *Vietnam: A Teacher's Guide.* New York: The Asia Society (725 Park Ave., New York, N.Y. 10021), 1983.

Boettcher, Thomas D. *Vietnam—The Valor and the Sorrow: From the Home Front to the Front Lines in Words and Pictures.* Boston: Little, Brown, 1985.

Bowman, John S., ed. *The World Almanac of the Vietnam War.* New York: Pharos, 1985.

Edelman, Bernard, ed. *Dear America: Letters Home from Vietnam.* New York: W. W. Norton, 1985.

Halberstam, David. *The Best and the Brightest.* New York: Random House, 1972.

Herr, Michael. *Dispatches.* New York: Alfred A. Knopf, 1978.

Herring, George C. *America's Longest War: The United States and Vietnam, 1950–1975.* New York: John Wiley & Sons, 1979.

Karnow, Stanley. *Vietnam: A History.* New York: Viking, 1983.

MacPherson, Myra. *Long Time Passing: Vietnam and the Haunted Generation.* New York: Doubleday, 1984.

Porter, Gareth, ed. *Vietnam: A History in Documents.* New York: New American Library, 1979.

Pratt, John Clark, ed. *Vietnam Voices: Perspectives on the War Years, 1941–1982.* New York: Penguin, 1984.

Sheehan, Neil, et al. *The Pentagon Papers.* New York: Bantam, 1971.

Truong, Nhu Tang. *A Viet Cong Memoir: An Inside Account of the Vietnam War and Its Aftermath.* New York: Harcourt Brace Jovanovich, 1985.

Oral Histories

Baker, Mark. *Nam: The Vietnam War in the Words of the Soldiers Who Fought There.* New York: William Morrow, 1981.

Beesley, Stanley W. *Vietnam: The Heartland Remembers.* Norman: University of Oklahoma Press, 1987.

Kimball, William R. *Vietnam: The Other Side of Glory.* Canton, Ohio: Daring, 1987.

Santoli, Al. *Everything We Had: An Oral History of the Vietnam War by Thirty-three American Soldiers Who Fought It.* New York: Oxford University Press, 1978.

Terry, Wallace. *Bloods: An Oral History of the Vietnam War by Black Veterans.* New York: Random House, 1984.

Willenson, Kim. *The Bad War: An Oral History of the Vietnam War.* New York: New American Library, 1987.

The Antiwar Movement

Halstead, Fred. *Out Now!: A Participant's Account of the American Movement Against the Vietnam War.* New York: Monad, 1978.

Mailer, Norman. *Armies of the Night.* New York: New American Library, 1968.

Powers, Thomas. *Vietnam: The War at Home—Vietnam and the American People, 1964–1968.* New York: Grossman, 1973.

Zaroulis, Nancy, and Gerald Sullivan. *Who Spoke Up? American Protest Against the War in Vietnam, 1963–1975.* New York: Holt, Rinehart & Winston, 1984.

Women in the War

Marshall, Kathryn. *In the Combat Zone: An Oral History of American Women in Vietnam, 1966–1975.* Boston: Little, Brown, 1987.

Van Devanter, Linda. *Home Before Morning: The Story of an Army Nurse in Vietnam.* New York: Warner, 1983.

Walker, Keith. *A Piece of My Heart: The Stories of Twenty-six Women Who Served in Vietnam.* Novato, Calif.: Presidio, 1985.

Fiction

Del Vecchio, John M. *The 13th Valley.* New York: Bantam, 1982.

Hasford, Gustav. *The Short-Timers.* New York: Harper & Row, 1979.

Heinemann, Larry. *Close Quarters.* New York: Farrar, Straus & Giroux, 1977.

Miller, Kenn. *Tiger the LURP Dog.* Boston: Little, Brown, 1983.

O'Brien, Tim. *Going After Cacciato.* New York: Delacorte, 1978.

Webb, James. *Fields of Fire.* Englewood Cliffs, N.J.: Prentice-Hall, 1978.